Talking on the Page:
Editing Aboriginal Oral Texts

The worlds of readers and writers on the one hand and listeners and speakers on the other differ in many ways. What happens when the stories, beliefs, or histories of North American Native people, many traditionally communicated orally, are transferred to paper or other media? Why do tellers, teachers, editors, filmmakers, and translators undertake this work? What do the words mean for different audiences? How can they be most effectively and responsibly presented and interpreted? This collection of essays confronts these and other issues that arise in attempting to record oral cultures for a visual society. The book contains an introduction by the editors, and papers by Nora Marks Dauenhauer and Richard Dauenhauer, Basil Johnston, Kimberly M. Blaeser, J. Edward Chamberlin, Victor Masayesva Jr., and Julie Cruikshank.

LAURA J. MURRAY is Assistant Professor, Department of English, Queen's University.

KEREN RICE is Professor, Department of Linguistics, University of Toronto.

Talking on the Page:
Editing Aboriginal Oral Texts

Papers given at the
Thirty-Second Annual Conference
on Editorial Problems
University of Toronto,
14–16 November 1996

Edited by Laura J. Murray and Keren Rice

UNIVERSITY OF TORONTO PRESS
Toronto Buffalo London

© University of Toronto Press Incorporated 1999
Toronto Buffalo London
Printed in Canada

ISBN 0-8020-4433-6 (cloth)
ISBN 0-8020-8230-0 (paper)

Printed on acid-free paper

Canadian Cataloguing in Publication Data

Conference on Editorial Problems (32nd : 1996 :
University of Toronto)
Talking on the page : editing aboriginal oral texts :
papers given at the thirty-second annual Conference
on Editorial Problems, University of Toronto,
14–16 November 1996

Includes bibliographical references.
ISBN 0-8020-4433-6 (bound); ISBN 0-8020-8230-0 (pbk.)

1. Oral tradition – North America – Congresses.
2. Oral history – Editing – Congresses. 3. Indians of
North America – Congresses. 4. Native peoples –
Canada – Congresses. I. Murray, Laura Jane, 1965– .
II. Rice, Keren Dichter, 1949– . III. Title

PN162.C64 1996   808'.06697   C98-932960–7

University of Toronto Press acknowledges
the financial assistance to its publishing program
of the Canada Council for the Arts and the Ontario
Arts Council.

Contents

Notes on Contributors

Kimberly M. Blaeser, Anishinaabe and an enrolled member of the Minnesota Chippewa Tribe from White Earth Reservation, is Associate Professor of English at the University of Wisconsin-Milwaukee, where she teaches courses in Native American Literature, creative writing, and natural history writing. Her publications include a collection of poetry, *Trailing You* (1994), which won the Diane Decorah First Book Award from the Native Writers' Circle of the Americas, and a critical study, *Gerald Vizenor: Writing in the Oral Tradition* (1996). Blaeser recently edited a collection of Anishinaabe prose, *Stories Migrating Home*, and her fiction, poetry, and scholarly and personal essays have appeared in over thirty Canadian and American collections.

J. Edward Chamberlin, Professor of English and Comparative Literature at the University of Toronto, is the author of *Come Back to Me My Language: Poetry and the West Indies* (1993). He served as Senior Research Associate with the Royal Commission on Aboriginal Peoples (1992–5), and has published widely on such varied subjects as Oscar Wilde, Aboriginal treaty rights, and postcolonial cultural studies. He is currently directing an international research project on oral and written traditions.

Julie Cruikshank is Professor in the Department of Anthropology and Sociology at the University of British Columbia. Her prize-winning *Life Lived Like a Story: Life Stories of Three Athapaskan Elders* (1990) has been considered a model of culturally sensitive collaborative oral history, and her articles have appeared in such journals as

Anthropology Today, Ethnohistory, Canadian Historical Review, and *Museum Anthropology.*

Nora Marks Dauenhauer (Tlingit) has co-authored many books and articles about Tlingit culture with Richard Dauenhauer, including the American Book Award–winning *Haa Tuwunáagu Yís/For Healing our Spirit: Tlingit Oratory* (1987); *Haa Kusteeyí/Our Culture: Tlingit Life Stories* (1990); and *Haa Shuká/Our Ancestors: Tlingit Oral Narratives* (1994). She is also well known for her poetry, some of which has been collected in *The Droning Shaman* (1988). Her latest book, *Life Woven with Song,* a collection of prose, poetry, and plays, will be published by University of Arizona Press in Spring 2000.

Richard Dauenhauer, formerly Program Director for Language and Cultural Studies at the Sealaska Heritage Foundation, is co-author with Nora Marks Dauenhauer of books and articles on Tlingit oratory and culture, some of which are mentioned above. He is widely recognized as a translator of poetry, and has served as Poet Laureate of Alaska.

Basil Johnston, a member of Cape Croker First Nation, has devoted his life to preserving and communicating Anishinaubae heritage. His many books include a memoir (*Indian School Days* [1988]), monographs on Anishinaubae culture (*The Manitous* [1995] and *Ojibway Heritage* [1976]), and illustrated collections of Anishinaubae stories (*The Bear Walker* [1995] and *Tales the Elders Told* [1981]). He is a member of the Order of Ontario and holds an honorary doctorate from the University of Toronto.

Victor Masayesva Jr., the owner of IS Productions, Inc., is the author with Erin Younger of *Hopi Photographers/Hopi Images* (1983). Among his sixteen films and videos, *Imagining Indians* (1994) was the first feature-length film produced and directed by a Native American; he has been artist-in-residence at several major art galleries and has won awards from several film festivals. His current work includes explorations of the media of photography and the Internet.

Laura J. Murray, Assistant Professor of English at Queen's University in Kingston, Ontario, is the editor of the diaries and letters of a Mohegan teacher, preacher, and political leader, *To Do Good to My Indian Brethren: The Writings of Joseph Johnson, 1751–1776* (1998).

Keren Rice is Professor of Linguistics at the University of Toronto. Her interest in aboriginal languages arose out of her work with the Dene languages of the Mackenzie River Valley, Canada. She is the author of *A Grammar of Slave* (1989), and of the forthcoming *Morpheme Order and Semantic Scope: Morpheme Order in the Athapaskan Verb*, among other works.

LAURA J. MURRAY AND KEREN RICE

Introduction

Mabel's story and conversation with Jenny – Mabel's talk – reminds us that in oral discourse the context of orality covers the personal territory of those involved in the exchange, and because the territory is so wide, extending throughout two or more personal, and often cultural, worlds, no one party has access to the whole of the exchange. One party may write a story, but one party's story is no more the whole story than a cup of water is the river. While this may seem obvious, it underscores what it is we do when we tell, transcribe, or write about oral texts. Basically, in whatever form or manner we deal with oral texts, whether orally or literally, we continue their life in very specific ways.

Greg Sarris, *Keeping Slug Woman Alive*

In adducing the words of Greg Sarris, a mixed-blood scholar and writer of Coast Miwok, Pomo, and Jewish descent, as an epigraph to our introduction, we both display and demonstrate his point. While without any intention to distort (quite the contrary), we have taken his words out of context, in distancing them from the story they comment on. The story in question is a layered one: Sarris tells of the misunderstandings that occurred when Mabel McKay, a Pomo teacher and Dreamer, told a story about a woman who loved a snake to a white graduate student in English. The widely differing cultural worlds Sarris refers to, then, are Mabel McKay's world, and the world of the graduate student. But in recounting the story – and the story of the story's telling – in a book, Sarris once again enlarges the number of worlds the story and story's story engage, including now his own and that of his various readers, and in quoting him here we do the same again. Each telling of a story, whether in speech or in writing, generates another story, a story of relations between people and their worlds.

A question then arises: are the relations between the worlds of readers and the worlds of writers different in kind from the relations between the worlds of listeners and the worlds of speakers? Many scholars and storytellers would say yes, but there would be a much wider range of opinion about how, why, and with what effect listeners are different from readers, or the listening experience different from the reading experience. One difference often cited lies in the level of immediacy. A speaker addressing a particular audience from one side of a room to another is performing a very different act from a writer publishing for an audience not only in another place, but perhaps even in another time. A speaker can see and hear those who are listening to her, and can elaborate or withhold information to suit that particular audience, whereas a writer can only speculate about the nature of an audience, its response and needs. A writer may meet none or only a few readers of his book, and those many years after the initial act of writing. Readers may attach experiences and meanings to his words such that he might hardly recognize his writing at all: Nathaniel Hawthorne, for example, could not have anticipated while writing *The Scarlet Letter* in the late 1840s that a hundred and fifty years later a student would read that novel as an allegory for her experience in suburban Toronto, growing up as the daughter of a single mother and a father both invasively present and unnervingly absent. Could they meet, Hawthorne and that student might well not agree about the most basic meanings of the novel. But in exchange for letting his words loose in the world, Hawthorne gained, of course, the power to reach many more people than an oral storyteller could.

There are middle grounds between the extremes of personal story-telling and published story-writing. If a speaker's words are recorded on tape or in writing and then published, the potential audience expands, and the layers of mediation between the words' sender and their receivers multiply from their original context. In many cases, the larger audience (or readership, really) does not know enough, or have a strong enough history of relation with the teller, to understand the story in the spirit it was told. But as Sarris points out in his example of Mabel McKay and the visiting graduate student, even the most intimate story-telling situation does not ensure identical understandings of a story. Even a grandmother and a grandchild within the same household experience the same story differently, as Basil Johnston observes in his contribution to this book, and in fact this ability to carry many meanings is a large part of the power of stories. We might add too that some kinds of writing – letters between friends or lovers, perhaps, or even the developing genre of email – are quite immediate in nature, and their emphasis on reciprocity and relationship may make them more akin to speech than to published books. Thoughts such as these make the difference between speech and writing seem less stark, and suggest that perhaps the difference we perceive lies more between mechanisms of publication and dissemination, and habits of interpretation we associate with them, than between spoken words and written words as such.

Many Native people fear the loss of control that comes with the reproduction of their words, on tape or on paper, because they have seen the dire legal effects of having their words misconstrued (or at least reconstrued with other people's interests in mind) in treaties and court decisions, and the crippling cultural effects of having their songs and histories reduced to quaint fairy tales or parables. The earliest European travellers to America often remarked upon the eloquence and authority of Native people's speech. But in seeking to fix Aboriginal speech into writing, these amanuenses and their successors did not only sacrifice accuracy (in many cases they did not speak the language of their Native interlocutors and depended upon interpreters with dubious skills), but they most often obscured indigenous interpretive frameworks, and the very life of the oral traditions themselves.[1] Operating in the 'salvage' mode, more recent non-Native amanuenses too have often taken oral traditions to be moribund or static that were in fact very much alive and various; they have often not known where to place any particular utterance in a universe of speech and culture. Some have even sought to hide the Aboriginal speaker's full range of expression and motivation, and the circumstances of 'collection' of the text. A famous example is *Black Elk Speaks* (Neihardt [1932] 1961), 'edited' by John G. Neihardt, who not only changed Black Elk's language and invented large parts of his story, but hid the fact that Black Elk was a Catholic catechist in order to maintain the mystique of the tragic medicine man, untouched by white ways (see DeMallie 1984; Couser 1989; Steltenkamp 1994).

During the past fifteen years or so, the work of Arnold Krupat (1985), Raymond DeMallie (1984), Barre Toelken and Tacheeni Scott (1981), and others has helped us to develop ways to 'read through' the manipulations of earlier editors so that we may gain some sense of meanings of the texts beyond what their editors understood. And furthermore, Aboriginal and non-Aboriginal linguists, anthropologists, poets, and storytellers – Dell Hymes (1981), Gerald Vizenor ([1965] 1993), Brian Swann (1994), and Dennis Tedlock (1983) were among the pioneers, and several of the authors in this book are at the forefront of this work – have been experimenting with diverse new ways of representing the spoken word of Aboriginal tradition. It has become more common to include framing material, almost like stage directions, to help the reader better re-create the actual storytelling situation; more amanuenses are also including in their books information about their own relation to the words and narratives, or their experience listening to and transcribing them. Increasing numbers of books present the text in two languages, with ragged right edges to show the rhythm of speech, and with commentary and artwork to make the stories accessible not only to scholars but to members of Native communities. Aboriginal novelists, playwrights, and poets are using writing not to freeze but to reanimate oral traditions. And alternative media, including video and hypertext technology, offer immense possibilities for stories to move back and forth between young and old, rural and urban, Native and non-Native.

For despite the risk of having their words transformed or interpreted beyond recognition, Aboriginal people may choose to disseminate those words because they have suffered from having the words of non-Native 'experts' valued over their own. Words not made public cannot serve to combat misunderstandings and ignorance in the general population; nor can they inform and encourage Native people living away from their elders in cities, or serve members of other Native groups who might welcome the stories and strategies of another culture by way of comparison. In the very act of writing and publishing, Greg Sarris joins many other Native authors in manifesting a hopeful sense that mediation's static does not have to drown out the telling. Sarris's sophisticated combination of story and argument suggests that it is in fact through awareness of mediation, of the nature of the relation between receivers, whoever they may be, and senders, that tellers can most effectively craft their words, and listeners and readers best hope to hear: the static becomes part of a larger multidimensional story, instead of a mask to an elusive, essential meaning.

It must however be acknowledged that such layering of stories in stories and performances in performances can be more arduous than exhilarating. An especially compelling example of the stakes of shifting the contexts of Aboriginal speech is the as-yet-unfinished story of the Gitksan and Wet'suwet'en land claims case, originally heard in British Columbia from 1987 to 1991, and discussed by Ted Chamberlin in his essay in this book. With few exceptions, British Columbia Native lands were never ceded by treaty, and the nature and boundaries of Aboriginal title are thus disputed there to an even greater extent than in other parts of North America. In the course of *Delgamuukw v. British Columbia*, the Gitksan and Wet'suwet'en people presented their traditional histories, which they know as *ada'ox* or *kungax*, as evidence of their continuous inhabitation of and relation to the land they claim as theirs. The courtroom enacted not only a translation from oral to written medium (all the names, stories, and songs had to be entered into the court record, which proved quite a challenge to the court reporters), but also a change in performance setting and audience, from one ritual space to another.[2] The plan to use the *ada'ox* and *kungax* as evidence was at first denied by the presiding judge on the grounds that oral history constituted hearsay. Although Justice McEachern reversed his ruling, and did listen to many hours, days, and weeks of traditional Gitksan and Wet'suwet'en history, he was apparently never able to *hear* this history, and the plaintiffs lost the case. But in December of 1997, the Supreme Court of Canada issued a judgment calling for a new trial (*Delgamuukw v. British Columbia* [1997] 3 S.C.R. 1010), saying that Justice McEachern had failed to make a correct finding of the facts of the case by devaluing the oral history. In discussing the judge's legal errors, Supreme Court Chief Justice Lamer observed that 'The implication of the trial judge's reasoning is that oral histories should never be given any independent weight and are only useful as confirmatory evidence in Aboriginal rights litigation. I fear that if this reasoning were followed, the oral histories of Aboriginal peoples would be consistently and systematically undervalued by the Canadian legal system, in contradiction of the express instruction to the contrary in Van der Peet that trial courts interpret the evidence of Aboriginal peoples in light of the difficulties inherent in adjudicating Aboriginal claims' (para. 98).

Whether the Gitksan and Wet'suwet'en will indeed pursue a new trial, or seek to resolve the land claim via negotiation, is not yet clear, and the larger legal implications of the Supreme Court's ruling are only beginning to be imagined, but clearly the *Delgamuukw* case is a landmark in the legitimation of the truth value of Aboriginal oral history, always previously valued far less highly by the courts than Euro-American or Euro-Canadian written history.[3] The *Delgamuukw* example speaks not only to the difficulty of transferring meaning from one context to another, but to the practical necessity of such attempts for the survival of First Nations communities. Stories are often not only the repository for a community's history, language, and cultural identity, but they also may serve as the crucial vehicle for its legal identity.

They may need to be conveyed in all sorts of different ways to all sorts of different audiences, from Native children to white judges. The stories' effectiveness in these varied venues depends not only on the power of the stories themselves, but on the shared commitment, creativity, and knowledge of tellers, mediators, and listeners.

The Conference on Editorial Problems at the University of Toronto, in 1996 in its thirty-second year, may at first blush seem like a strange venue to discuss issues such as these. But as the convenors of the 1996 conference, we took the word 'edit' to mean 'make public' or 'prepare for publication,' and thus we understood a wide variety of activities and responsibilities to fall within the purview of editing. Even a storyteller him- or herself is thus an editor, shaping material in particular ways for a particular public, as Julie Cruikshank emphasizes in her contribution to this book. Transcription, translation, page and book design, and annotation, are all part of the editing process, as is choice of medium among the proliferating options of books, film and video, websites, and CD-ROMs. Approaches to each of these aspects of editing, broadly conceived, often depend on immediate factors such as availability of time, money, and dedicated and suitable listener-transcribers – as Nora and Richard Dauenhauer's essay reminds us particularly vividly. But larger questions are also inescapable. Who is the intended audience? Young people within the community, academics, and non-Native general readers, for example, would have different expectations and needs in terms of annotation and design. What is the purpose of reaching this audience? One might seek to teach, to document, to inspire, to amuse, or some of each, and the particular combination determines the choice of stories and perhaps even tellers, as well as the format in which they are presented. And what rhetorical strategy will achieve this purpose? Sometimes audiences might best be made comfortable with what might otherwise be culturally alienating material; other times it might be most effective to force their discomfort, so they appreciate the cultural distances they are being asked to travel. It is up to the editor and designer, as well as the teller, to create such effects.

Such decisions are not dissimilar to those faced by an editor of any oral texts, or even written texts. Other volumes in this series have explored the variety of goals and methods editors have employed with respect to maps, music, drama, poetry, and many other genres in many historical periods. Articles within these volumes have demonstrated that written texts are often not as fixed as we might suppose them to be. And as the difficulties in comprehending the nature and authority of oral texts are not entirely distinct from those that arise with respect to written texts, it can also be noted that questions that arise with respect to Native North American oral traditions are not entirely different from those addressed in discussions of other oral traditions, as several of our contributors note. Nonetheless, as we have already pointed out, in the context of the history of the misrepresentation or silencing of Native speech that has characterized so much of colonial history in North America, editorial decisions about the representation of Native people's spoken words bear a particular urgency, difficulty, and weight.

It was thus a broad complex of practical, historical, theoretical, artistic, and ethical concerns that we sought to address at Talking on the Page: Editing Aboriginal Oral Texts, a conference held at University College of the University of Toronto on 14, 15, and 16 November 1996. As we planned the conference, we sent each speaker the following questions to keep in mind during the preparation of their presentation:

- What happens when the spoken word is transferred to paper?
- What are the reasons for writing down Aboriginal words, on the part of the speaker, and on the part of the editor or amanuensis? How does the intended audience affect the way we approach the project?
- How can we do a better job in this translation? Can non-written modes of reproduction and transmutation – storytelling, film, or drama, for example – be more faithful to the original, more effective, or more creative?

And more fundamentally,

- What is the importance and structure of speech in Aboriginal societies, and can (or should) that importance be communicated in other media and contexts?

The conference sought to allow people from across the continent to talk in one room about editing Aboriginal speech. Speakers were both Native and non-Native, independent scholars and writers as well as university professors, and they came from as far away as Peace River, Alberta; Juneau, Alaska; and Hotevilla, Arizona – and as nearby as Toronto and Cape Croker, Ontario. One speaker, Victor Masayesva, is a filmmaker (he is also a poet and photographer); others are anthropologists, poets, playwrights, literary scholars, and in most cases more than one of these. Most of the speakers are also editors, in one sense or another.

This book effects a transformation from the conference setting to the page, with many of the attendant problems and advantages our speakers/authors address in their papers. Without their original audience, these papers lose a certain immediacy, and they lack the buzz of discussion during coffee breaks, or the hush in the auditorium during, for example, Maria Campbell's electrifying presentation. In fact, Campbell's words themselves have not made the transition to this book in any form, a loss which we greatly regret. The papers are presented here too without the framing of welcomes and thanks by Lillian McGregor, Jon Cohen, and Robert Pritchard. You as readers, however, share the responsibility of the audience at the conference: you will 'listen with your eyes' and compare to your own experience and study. Those who spoke at the conference in Toronto can speak to many more through the written word than they did in that one room.

If we take this book to be something of a case study of interfaces between speaking and writing, it is interesting to consider that even the original conference presentations were quite hybrid in nature. Although Ted Chamberlin read a prepared text, it was quite 'oral' in quality, as you will see when you read its opening. Kim Blaeser offered a seamless blend of reading and ad-libbing; if she had not told us afterwards that the original written text did not include many of the links and conclusions she presented in her talk, we would never have known. Maria Campbell and Nora and Richard Dauenhauer frequently and overtly departed from prepared parts of their texts; Campbell chose not to send a written version for the book at all whereas the Dauenhauers' words multiplied on paper. Basil Johnston and Victor Masayesva (who also presented two films) spoke with little reference to notes, and both have chosen to create new works for this book that touch on related themes to their presentations at the conference, but that do not pretend to replicate those presentations. Thus the relation between speech and print was as various in the talks as it is in the papers, and as it was at the reading at Toronto's Native Canadian Centre the first night of the conference, when Kim Blaeser read from her poetry, Maria Campbell read from written versions of what she calls 'stories of the road allowance people,' and Nora Dauenhauer read poetry and also (with the assistance of Richard Dauenhauer) transcriptions of traditional Tlingit ceremonial speech.

Nora Marks Dauenhauer and Richard Dauenhauer have worked for many years to document Alaskan Tlingit oral culture. We have placed their essay first, because for readers about to embark upon recording Aboriginal spoken texts, or who are not experienced in thinking about the mechanics behind oral materials they read, this is a truly encyclopedic introduction. It includes discussion of the largest philosophical and political issues, most specific practical concerns, and most intimate personal motivations involved in transcribing traditional Aboriginal narratives. Based mainly on the authors' experience with Tlingit-language materials, the article also develops a comparison with Richard Dauenhauer's recent work with Charles Natkong, Sr, transcribing and translating already-existing Haida-language tapes. The Dauenhauers conclude with some thought-provoking meditations on the cultural and political differences between the generations of Tlingit about the best way to preserve or revivify traditional culture.

Basil Johnston's presentation at the conference, while interrupted by microphone feedback and the clink of cutlery, was marked by his sparkling humour and his rich experience as an interpreter of Anishinaubae culture to non-Native people and young Native people. For the book, he has decided to address more particularly the teaching of Aboriginal languages. We learn language, Johnston argues, not by thinking about its structure, but by listening for sound and story; language only matters because it communicates knowledge from one person to another. And we learn the messages of stories not from explicit explanations of them, but because of their comic situations and essential humanity. These facts, demonstrated in Johnston's essay with Anishinaubae stories, call for a more holistic approach for the teaching and preservation of Aboriginal languages and traditions than is often practiced. Preservation of Native languages is, according to Johnston, not only impossible, but pointless, if it does not proceed by way of talking and storytelling.

Kimberly Blaeser's article, like Johnston's, insists on the centrality of stories to Native American life as it explores the relation between oral tradition and contemporary Native literature. Following Gerald Vizenor, Blaeser suggests that while Native oratory may not really be able to be translated, it can be 'reimagined.' The writing of Betty Bell, Anna Lee Walters, Simon Ortiz, and others, is characterized, according to Blaeser, by a foregrounded demand for reciprocity with its readers, similar to the way traditional stories engage their listeners. Like Native stories, Native-authored books depend upon readers' efforts to complete and complement their meanings; in making such efforts, readers themselves join in the creation and maintenance of a vital Native culture.

Ted Chamberlin is also a literary scholar; his wide-ranging paper circles around the importance of form and genre. He suggests that confronting a text whose ways of establishing truth are not familiar should cause a listener a moment of *non*sense; and that without ac-knowledgment of such disorientation, comprehension cannot happen. But the solution is not to make all stories and histories fit the same formal template. Chamberlin argues (using poetry and riddles as examples, and drawing on his experience with the Aboriginal History Project of Canada's Royal Commission on Aboriginal Peoples) that getting Aboriginal history right is not so much a matter of correcting facts, but a matter of teaching more people to hear previously marginalized *ways* of talking about the past.

In his contribution to the volume, Victor Masayesva, Jr, a Hopi film-maker, discusses the difficulties he faces in his work: not only is it extremely difficult to translate the Hopi world-view accurately to non-Hopis, but many Hopis do not think such translation should be at-tempted in the first place. Masayesva discusses language and culture as a sovereignty issue – a perspective clearly continuous with those raised by earlier papers in the book. Masayesva is concerned that out-siders not control language and its dissemination, but he also suggests that as sovereignty is experienced only partially by Native people, so is Native language, in a world where English, at least for younger gen-erations, is an inescapable part of life. Neither political sovereignty nor linguistic competence can be accomplished by proclamation alone, so individuals and communities must constantly defend, negotiate, and accommodate.

Like Masayesva, the Yukon Native women Julie Cruikshank has worked with are pragmatic in their approach to preserving and con-veying their culture, but it appears that they are more comfortable than he in their mediating roles. Cruikshank, an anthropologist, suggests that we think of the decision of these women to tell their stories in English not so much as a loss but as a choice: the women want their grandchildren, who learn from books, to learn from their stories; and furthermore, Cruikshank argues that the English-language stories they tell are much richer in style and idiom than they would have been had they been told in a Native language and then translated. These story-tellers, Cruikshank says, are not only translators, but editors, as they adapt their spoken stories, and even reanimate written versions of their stories in different contexts. Cruikshank closes with some provocative questions about the legal and political implications of oral history work in Aboriginal communities.

Talking on the Page in either conference or book form could not have happened could without help from many quarters. Many thanks to Ann Hutchison and Gillian Fenwick for early help with grants and logistics, and to Maria Leonor Cunha, John Grant, and Don Moggridge for helping us keep track of money. For information, inspiration, and elbow-grease, thanks to Jean Balcaen, Anita Benedict, Rodney Bobiwash, Saradindu Guha, Lillian McGregor, Monica McKay, Ted Chamberlin, and Suzanne Rancourt. Albert Braz, Ed Doolittle, Barbara Gajic, Deirdre Kwiatek, Margaret McGeachy, Stephanie McKenzie, and Carolyn Podruchny served as poised and intelligent moderators. Rodney Bobiwash, Trudy Nicks, Krystyna Sieciechowicz, and Paul Seesequasis offered eloquent end-of-conference responses. For facilitating the final production of the book, we thank Kristen Pederson and Barb Porter at University of Toronto Press.

For financial support, we are extremely grateful to the Social Sciences and Humanities Research Council of Canada, and, at the University of Toronto, the Connaught Fund, the School of Graduate Studies, the Department of English, the Faculty of Arts & Science, University College, Cinema Studies, the American Studies Committee, University of Toronto Press, First Nations House, and the Department of Linguistics.

NOTES

1 Two (in)famous examples of highly mediated and perhaps apocryphal recorded Native American speech are the 1774 speech of Chief Logan, and what might be called the 'environmentalist' 1854 speech of Chief Seattle. See Jefferson ([1784] 1955); Seeber (1947); Low (1995).

2 Monet and Skanu'u (1992) have created a rich scrapbook account of the experience of the original trial, including cartoons and local newspaper clippings; the introductory material to Mills (1994) surveys McEachern's attitudes and ruling; for a poetic meditation on what the judgment says about the legal profession, see Pinder (1991). Gray (1998) provides useful information and speculation about the effects of the 1997 Canadian Supreme Court ruling.

3 Ted Chamberlin has observed, however (personal communication, July 1998), that the language of the 1997 ruling continues to essentialize oral tradition in a way that will work against the *Delgamuukw* decision and permit continued denigration and misunderstanding of traditional forms of Aboriginal history.

WORKS CITED

Couser, G. Thomas. 1989. 'Black Elk Speaks with Forked Tongue,' in *Altered Egos: Authority in American Autobiography*. New York: Oxford University Press.

DeMallie, Raymond. 1984. *The Sixth Grandfather*. Lincoln: University of Nebraska Press.

Gray, John. 1998. 'Laying Claim: The Historic Delgamuukw Decision.' *The Globe and Mail*, June 6, 8, and 9.

Hymes, Dell. 1981. *In Vain I Tried to Tell You: Essays in Native American Ethnopoetics*. Philadelphia: University of Pennsylvania Press.

Jefferson, Thomas. [1784] 1955. *Notes on the State of Virginia*. Ed. William Peden. Chapel Hill: University of North Carolina Press.

Krupat, Arnold. 1985. *For Those Who Come After: A Study of Native American Autobiography*. Berkeley: University of California Press.

Low, Denise. 1995. 'Contemporary Reinvention of Chief Seattle: Variant Texts of Chief Seattle's 1854 Speech.' *American Indian Quarterly* 19.

Mills, Antonia. 1994. *Eagle Down is Our Law: Witsuwit'en Law, Feasts, and Land Claims*, 407–21. Vancouver: University of British Columbia Press.

Monet, Don, and Skanu'u (Ardythe Wilson). 1992. *Colonialism on Trial: Indigenous Land Right and the Gitksan and Wet'suwet'en Sovereignty Case*. Gabriola Island: New Society.

Neihardt, John G. [1932] 1961. *Black Elk Speaks*. Lincoln: University of Nebraska Press.

Pinder, Leslie. 1991. *The Carriers of No: After the Land Claims Trial*. Vancouver: Lazara.

Sarris, Greg. 1993. *Keeping Slug Woman Alive: A Holistic Approach to American Indian Texts*. Berkeley: University of California Press.

Seeber, Edward D. 1947. 'Critical Views on Logan's Speech.' *Journal of American Folklore* 60: 130–46.

Steltenkamp, Michael. 1994. *Black Elk: Holy Man of the Oglala*. Norman: University of Oklahoma Press.

Swann, Brian, ed. 1994. *Coming to Light: Contemporary Translations of Native Literatures of North America*. New York: Random House.

Tedlock, Dennis. 1983. *The Spoken Word and the Work of Interpretation*. Philadelphia: University of Pennsylvania Press.

Toelken, Barre, and Tacheeni Scott. 1981. 'Poetic Retranslation and the "Pretty Languages" of Yellowman,' in *Traditional American Indian Literatures*, edited by Karl Kroeber, 65–116. Lincoln: University of Nebraska Press.

Vizenor, Gerald. [1965] 1993. *Summer in the Spring: Anishinaabe Lyric Poems and Stories, New Edition*. Norman: University of Oklahoma Press.

Talking on the Page

NORA MARKS DAUENHAUER
AND RICHARD DAUENHAUER

1 The paradox of talking on the page: Some aspects of the Tlingit and Haida experience

This is a conference about oral texts, so we have allowed ourselves some oral comments as context for the written paper. First of all, we thank Keren Rice and Laura Murray, our colleagues in the Canadian connection, for organizing this conference, and for inviting us to be a part of it. Being here on stage reminds us that it is easier for us to talk about our work than to write it or write about it; and it's easier to write it than to read it. We've figured out how to co-author; but we haven't figured out how to co-read. The poet Theodore Roethke said (or wrote) someplace that a teacher is a person who carries out his or her education in public. So, it's good to be here and to carry on the public education of ourselves in the college of co-readership.

We are excited by the juncture of oral and written literature. All of the Great Literatures of the world began at that point. For the Western cultural tradition this includes Beowulf, the Homeric epics, and ancient Hebrew literature. These began as oral traditions that were written down as literacy entered the cultures. Eventually, composition in writing began as a process different from oral composition and the transcription of oral texts (Lord 1991, esp. chaps. 1, 2). For the indigenous literatures of North America – called Native American literature in the United States, and First Nations literature in Canada – that's where we are now. Conference participants heard samples of all the components at the reading last night: creative writing in English by Maria Campbell, Kim Blaeser (1994), and Nora Marks Dauenhauer (1988, 1991); oral tradition in the local English dialect of the community (the wholly owned, self-governed dialect often called, for want of better terms, 'Indian English,' 'Village English,' or 'non-standard English') given a literary life by Maria Campbell (1995); and Tlingit ceremonial oratory transcribed in Tlingit and translated into English by

Nora Marks Dauenhauer (1990). This is a very exciting period for the indigenous oral and written literatures of North America. But it is also a period not without confusion, anxiety, and trauma. We'll be touching on all of these as we report on our experiences transcribing, translating, and publishing Tlingit and Haida oral literature from Alaska. We will not address Aboriginal texts composed in writing, nor will we discuss the additional dimension of computer applications such as interactive programs combining the transcribed texts, graphics, reference files, and the original sound recordings. Nor will we go into detail about our sixteen-or-so year history of modifying computer hardware and software for fluent word processing, screen display, printing, and electronic mail transmission of texts using character sets other than standard English.

After our first book, we were asked by so many readers as well as by our editors to explain who does what that we added a section to the introduction of the second book (1990: xvii–xx). Basically, the final product is approved by both co-authors, but separate parts of it originate with one or the other. For our co-authored books, Nora (as the native speaker of Tlingit) is the principal fieldworker and usually drafts the Tlingit transcriptions, English translations, and cultural annotations. Nora also conducts the genealogical and biographical research. After some discussion, Richard usually drafts the research aspects such as the introduction, and the linguistic annotations. Then we discuss and argue over the drafts created by each partner, a process which typically creates considerable marital discord and often brings us to the brink of divorce. For the present paper, both co-authors contributed written sections and discussion, based upon which Richard wrote the first draft, primarily because he writes and types faster in English than Nora.

We would like to close these opening remarks by expressing our gratitude to the Tlingit elders who encouraged us and supported our work. Most of them are now departed, but we remain forever thankful for their guidance and direction. These elders put their faith in Nora as a Tlingit person, and accepted Richard as an outsider and a newcomer, trusting us with their literary and cultural inheritance. Some of these elders were also politically active, and went to bat for us in forming Sealaska Heritage Foundation as a home for this kind of work. It took courage for them to take these risks on our behalf, so it is always appropriate for us to dedicate this paper to their collective memory, and to take the time to thank them as a pivotal and seminal generation in the history of Tlingit literature. These elders include

George Davis, David Kadashan, William Johnson, Jessie Dalton, Susie James, Robert Zuboff, J.B. Fawcett, Austin Hammond, Amy Marvin, Katherine Mills, Charlie Joseph, Jennie Marks, and many, many others, including Nora's parents, Willie and Emma Marks.

1 Introduction

In looking at what happens to oral texts as we write them down and publish them, it seems best to us to address first the more technical aspects of how we create a written text from an oral performance. Then, having established that text, we can examine the differing emotional reactions to it, both from people within the culture and without. Finally, we can review the personal delights and dilemmas of the work and address the question of why we do it. We will draw primarily from anecdotal material from our quarter century of teaching and fieldwork in Alaska, especially with Tlingit, and more recently with Haida.

Our teamwork has resulted in the publication of an ongoing series with the University of Washington Press called *Classics of Tlingit Oral Literature*. Three volumes have appeared to date, one each on prose narrative, ceremonial oratory, and life history (Dauenhauer and Dauenhauer 1987, 1990, 1994); and we have two additional volumes nearing completion, one of Tlingit Raven stories, and one of historical oral and written traditions pertaining to Tlingit-Russian relations and focussing in particular on the Battles of Sitka of 1802 and 1804. Each genre poses unique textual, contextual, and cultural problems for its editors. Our goal has always been to produce high quality transcriptions and translations of texts from the moribund Tlingit oral tradition, and to do so in a manner culturally acceptable to the Tlingit people, technically acceptable to the scholarly community, and stylistically accessible to the general public (who we think of as the interested, intelligent reader). This is not always easy, because the three constituencies often have differing attitudes, assumptions, and expectations regarding such work, and there may also be disagreement among various members of the same constituency according to generational or other subgrouping (Dauenhauer and Dauenhauer 1995, 1997). Most recently, we are encountering new concepts of political correctness from the middle-aged Tlingit generation whose attitudes are noticeably different from the elders on the one hand, and the youth and young adults on the other. These can be explained to some extent by differing generational experience with the traditional language and culture and with an English and larger Euro-American worldview. Moreover, oral and written literature do not share the same set of aesthetic values regarding composition, publication, and audience appreciation. As A.B. Lord describes it, 'The editing process itself ... argues the existence of two poetics at odds with one another ... The editor and the singer [have] different ideas of what constitute an acceptable poetics' (1991, 125). At all levels, oral and written literature are contextualized differently.

We have operated on the periphery of Haida work since the early 1970s, but have engaged in text work intermittently at best. In 1996 we began working with Mr Charles Natkong, Sr, of Hydaburg, on a project to bring his collection of Haida transcriptions into published form. At the age of sixty-seven, Natkong is the youngest speaker of Haida in Alaska. The total number of Haida speakers in Alaska and Canada combined is now estimated at no more than eighty. (Numbers for Tlingit are more difficult to compile, but nine hundred is a generous estimate, and six hundred perhaps closer to reality.) Natkong worked with linguists Michael Krauss and Jeff Leer on a number of transcriptions in the early 1970s, but these were never developed or edited further for publication. Although Natkong is the most competent Native-speaking Haida transcriber, with considerable training in Haida linguistics, he had no previous exposure to the folklore aspects of preparing texts for translation in bilingual editions. Our project has been to work with him in editing the Haida transcriptions, and in developing English translations and annotations. This experience has been helpful for us as a 'refresher.' As we apply old methods to a new field, we learn something in the process and take notice of things we take for granted in our Tlingit work because of long familiarity.

2 Decisions involved in obtaining the original text

In the introduction to our first volume (1987), we discussed how at each stage of the recording and documentation of oral literature, something gets lost as the dynamics move from performance to the printed page. Even on videotape, it is difficult to capture the total relationship of the storyteller to his or her audience. With audiotape, all of the gestures are lost. We no longer know what the storyteller looks like, and how he or she uses facial expressions and other body language to tell the story. When the story is written down, we lose everything about the voice. We don't know how the storyteller sounds. We can't hear the change of voice or delivery for different characters in dialogue. When the Native-language text is translated into English, we lose the original language, the way the storyteller put his or her words together to create a special and unique performance, an event that will never be repeated. We lose the style or 'texture' of the original (Dundes 1964, Toelken 1976). Even if the story is told over and over, it is never exactly the same, because the conditions are different, and the audience is different. In oral performance, there is no fixed or standard text (Bailey 1995; Lord 1965, 1991, 1995). The print form creates permanence and standardization not characteristic of the folklore dynamics. And then when the story is read by a person outside the culture of the storyteller, the cultural context is lost. Information and assumptions shared by the tradition-bearer and original audience may no longer be shared. Despite this inevitable loss, there are ways we can try our best to retain or re-create on the written page as much as we can of the original performance.

A description of fieldwork and problems of obtaining the tape recording for the text in the first place are beyond the scope of this paper, as are topics such as the care and archiving of tapes.[1] Rather, we would like to touch on a few aspects of the oral performance context that tend to influence important editorial decisions about which oral versions are selected as 'best,' and which are rejected as inferior, or simply overlooked. As a rule of thumb, we have observed that oral literature performance is highly situational and contextualized. To the extent that shared knowledge between the performer and the audience is assumed by the performer, it is not made explicit in the performance. This generally means that the more the fieldworker knows, the less detail will be explicit in the story. The less the fieldworker knows, the more information will be explicit. In situations where we have versions of the same story by the same storyteller, one told in English to a younger fieldworker, the other in Haida or Tlingit to an older fieldworker, the Native-language version will be more implicit and laconic, the English version more explicit and detailed. The question arises: what is a 'good' or 'best' version, and how does one get it? Outsiders tend to find the versions with most explanation and detail to be most satisfying and coherent. From the indigenous point of view, the best versions are the most laconic. Teachers in one rural Alaska district were frustrated at Athabaskan students' seeming inability or unwillingness to offer detailed retellings of events, but were amazed by the students' skill at 'writing précis' (Scollon and Scollon 1984). It is important to be aware of this tendency, and how it relates to cultural values regarding literary taste. It is also very important to note that most 'retellings' of Native stories aimed at English-language readers tend to be overstated in style. Even when the stories are written by members of the indigenous community, and the content may be traditional, the style may be Western and consciously or unconsciously geared to the cultural, educational, and market tastes of the dominant society. A recent example from Alaska is *Two Old Women* by Velma Wallis (1993): the book is very accessible and very popular, probably because is is Euro-American-English in style.

Where we have different versions, which version is 'correct'? As noted above, most specialists in oral literature emphasize that there is no single 'correct' version in oral literature (Lord 1965, 3–8, 100; 1995, 212–13). In contrast to a fixed text, we should expect variation among versions by different tradition-bearers as well as from one performance to another by the same tradition-bearer. This is well described by James Bailey:

> Perhaps the most important difference, and the most difficult one for
> literary scholars to comprehend, is that the text of a folk song
> 'lives' in variants. There is no single fixed text once and for all,
> but rather an open-ended series of variants, a feature which arises
> from the very essence of folk songs as an oral literature. The verbal
> text of a folk song not only differs from singer to singer, but also
> varies from performance to performance even by the same singer.
> Each published version of a folk song therefore represents a unique
> realization recorded on a single occasion. Succinctly stated, the
> fluidity of the oral text is opposed to the fixity of the written text
> (1995, 474).

One of the first editors in the Western tradition to encounter the dilemma of variants was the 'Priestly' editor of Genesis, who had to deal with two divinely inspired but differing versions of creation! An early editor also had to solve the problem of culturally embarassing material such as bride-rape and the episode of the Levite's concubine (Judges 19). In other words, these editorial problems have been with us for a long time. Our solution is to recognize the uniqueness and independence of each performance, and to transcribe, translate, and publish them as distinct versions (see Dauenhauer and Dauenhauer 1987). Others may choose to combine versions to create a more 'generic,' and perhaps more 'complete,' version. Historically, this may account for the extraordinary length of the Homeric epics. Recently and closer to home, our colleagues with the Naa Kahidi Theater in Juneau have used this technique, working with several versions and several elders to create a dramatic version for public performance that combines theatrical elements of both Northwest-coast and Western tradition.

Another feature of style that we note in virtually all Tlingit oral performances, but in few if any of the published English versions, is what we call a narrative frame (R. Dauenhauer 1975, 1976). The narrative frame is a kind of preface in which the storyteller somehow identifies him- or herself, traces knowledge of the story from a reliable source, asserts the right to transmit the story, and in other ways establishes the context for and validity of the performance. We consider it important to include such frames in the transcription, although most previous editors have deleted them as unimportant or extraneous. Our inclusion of the frames was visibly appreciated by all the elders with whom we have worked as an indication that the transcription was accurate and not a rewrite or paraphrase. It is also important to note that on occasions when we have heard the same story told by the same elder under different conditions, the 'story proper' was largely unchanged in general style and content (although in some cases a motif or two may have been added or deleted) but the narrative frames differed greatly, according to context.[2]

We have noted one major change in taste among certain elders over the last twenty-five years. The traditional preference seems to have been for the story 'itself' with minimal editorial comment. Requests for clarification even frustrated some storytellers. When asked a question about a story, one tradition-bearer routinely answered with another story, often equally enigmatic to a beginner. The tendency among some elders now is just the opposite, and may consist of 90 per cent comment and 10 per cent story in a self-conscious effort to preach to the younger generation. The traditional style was understated and laconic, allowing the tradition to speak for itself, with minimal intrusion by the storyteller and maximum freedom for the listener to make sense of it for him- or herself (Swann 1994; Toelken 1976, 1987, 1994). The traditional style was opposite to that of the Western sermon or essay; the new style, however, is quite similar, being self-consciously pedagogical, explicit, and didactic. Also, stories are being told increasingly in English, rather than in Tlingit or Haida. At the same time, we have also observed a general shift in language patterns toward what Craig calls 'use of language not for communication but as a phatic gesture of ethnic identity' (1992, 22). Finally, we should note that most recorded versions of Aboriginal prose narrative today are probably from an unnatural setting – that of tradition-bearer speaking privately or in a small group to a fieldworker with a tape recorder – because the opportunities for natural tale-telling situations are greatly reduced. In contrast, oratory is still easily recorded in performance in a natural setting of public speaking to a live audience. Context should be kept in mind to the extent that it is usually related to style.

3 Transcription and editing

Let us assume now that we have a tape and have selected it to work with. The first step is to make a copy and work from the copy, not the original. Tapes can break or convert to 'spaghetti,' and it is better for this to happen to a copy than to the only original! We are now ready to transcribe. The most fundamental aspect of our work, transcription from a tape recording, is by no means understood in a single way. When we first began working with Alaska Native students over twenty-five years ago, we noticed a tendency for them to listen to the original, write it down in English translation, and then back-translate into the Native language. The resulting text is a paraphrase rather than a transcription. In fact, we have observed it to be extremely difficult for beginning transcribers of all ages and in various languages to transcribe Native-language material directly to the page. We believe this is because literacy is associated with English for many speakers of indigenous languages (Scollon and Scollon 1981); the concept of direct transcription or original written composition in a Native language is usually alien. Ralph Maud's work (1989, 1993; R. Dauenhauer 1994a) based on Henry Tate's original manuscripts shows that this process frustrated Boas almost a century ago. It now seems that many of the classic Tsimshian texts published by Boas were not first written or transcribed in Tsimshian, but were composed in English and then translated into Tsimshian – and are therefore essentially classics of creative writing in English! Since this tendency is alive and well among all beginners with whom we have worked, it is important to be sure that the actual words of the storyteller are being written down directly, as told by the storyteller, in the storyteller's dialect. If the editor or transcriber takes issue with the storyteller, the place to deal with it is usually in notes. We also frequently encounter confusion between the terms 'transcription' and 'translation.' By 'transcription,' we mean to write down from an oral source in the language in which it is spoken. By 'translation,' we mean to carry the transcribed text in the original language over into another language.

We will discuss translation below, but we begin by discussing the endpoint: the formatting of the text. The most immediately noticeable feature of our transcriptions is the short line format. In this we follow the lead suggested by Tedlock (1983) that is now commonly accepted in ethnopoetic work. In the short line format, a new line marks a significant pause in delivery. This may or may not correspond to the grammatical unit, depending on whether a sentence ending is followed by a pause, or 'run on' in the oral delivery – a common device associated with heightened dramatic action. An elaboration of this format has been suggested by Dell Hymes (1981, 1989), in which the lines are further arranged by a pattern of indentation and spacing to signify scenes and acts. We do not use this format, not because we disagree with it, but because it requires additional time-consuming analysis of the text. Line turnings are relatively easy to hear because they reflect breath units and pauses in the oral delivery and require editorial judgment calls only in exceptional cases; but division into acts and scenes requires an editorial judgment and conceptual overlay on the text that we are not yet comfortable making. But we encourage Hymes and others to apply this kind of reading to our texts and trans-lations.

In the twenty-five years that we have been using it, we have found the short line format convenient. The page layout allows for a reading that approximates the original delivery, and the spacing is 'user-friendly' for beginning literacy in the indigenous languages. The only question the method invites is how much detail to note, and this will always be an editorial decision. Published examples from different traditions show different editorial taste and levels of detail. Loudness and softness can be marked by different point sizes in print; asides and audience reaction can be noted in brackets, italics, etc.[3] In general, we have kept our transcription simple, preferring to put details on deli-very in the annotations (for example, when the storyteller speaks in different voices for each character).

Let us now step back from the appearance of the text and examine how we get from the tape to a formatted text. Our rule of thumb is to transcribe everything, by hand, at the level of the first, rough draft. At the first editing and proofreading, we tend to edit out any stutterings and false starts. We feel it is not important to include the false starts, but we do like to mention in the notes those places in the text where they have been edited out. It is important to be careful, because in some places it may be unclear if a word is a false start or if in fact it functions as part of literary repetition.

We have observed over the years a tendency of beginning transcribers to delete repetitions. Some of our colleagues unfamiliar with the style of oral literature have even denounced certain storytellers as being drunk because they repeated themselves. We have discussed repetition in Tlingit at some length in the introductions to our books (1987, 1990) so we won't repeat it here. We note only that repetition as an organizational feature is universal in oral composition. Different traditions share many kinds of complete and partial repetition: 'terracing,' for example (with one line building on the wording of the previous line), and parallel structure (familiar from Biblical poetry). Repetition is the underlying concept in formulaic composition of epic poetry, and it operates similarly in North American prose traditions that are not strictly formulaic because they are not composed in a fixed metrical verse unit.

We have also noted a purist reaction against code-switching, or mixing English words in with the Native language. Here folklorists and linguists sometimes come into conflict. Some of our linguist colleagues prefer to edit out code-switching. There is a tendency to edit out the English entirely where it echoes a word or phrase in the Native language, and to replace English words with Native words where they do not pattern in repetition. Our preference is to transcribe the code-switching because it conveys the storyteller's personality, style, and point of view. These are important folklore considerations. At times, for pedagogical reasons, we have restored Tlingit words in a text, but we have identified such places in the notes.

In other words, the primary message in teaching transcription is, write down faithfully what is there, in the words of the storyteller. It is also important to use the dialect and pronunciation of the storyteller. All of these things mark the uniqueness of the performance and clearly identify the source as personal and not generic. This is not always easy, especially if the voice or dialect is unfamiliar, or if there is ambient noise on the tape. Some places on a tape may be difficult or even impossible to hear. In this case, the only way to get it is to listen over and over. Sometimes we simply have to guess. Unclear or restored passages can be identified in the notes.

It is good to transcribe and then translate as soon as possible, especially if the storyteller is still alive. Questions will invariably arise in the transcription or translation, and it is far easier and more valuable to clarify these issues with the collaboration of the storyteller. Our current Haida project involves stories recorded in the early 1970s from elders who are no longer alive. Even elders now in their eighties do not know about half of the vocabulary items in question.

Somewhere in these early stages we type or word process the handwritten transcription. This presents two problems. We have found it very hard to find good typists for languages other than English. In our experience, amateurs have proven best. They are slower, but they read their work as they go, a process professionals are trained not to do. Horror stories abound among linguists of the number of errors per page introduced by professional typists and typesetters. Each new generation of text must be carefully checked against the previous copy. Recent advances in computer technology have greatly helped in this regard. On the other hand, most computer software in the United States is almost hopelessly monolingual English. Major advances have been made in recent years over the early computers, but it is still difficult on some systems to achieve fluent word processing, printing, and electronic mail transfer using character sets other than standard English. (Canadian software is a little more progressive regarding bilingualism, but we still have a long way to go toward computer fluency for indigenous languages.) We should note here that some people may prefer to word process directly from the tape, but most of the people we know prefer pencil or pen – the darker the better for the purpose of making copies – for the first draft.

Here we should mention some other technical and practical aspects of the work. For ease in editing and proofreading, we double space the manuscripts. We also use and encourage others to use the accepted standard orthography for writing the languages. Unfortunately, there is still resistance in some quarters to learning and using standard orthography. Some people are eager to write down local traditions, but are not willing to learn and use a standard orthography. Whereas literacy is perceived by teachers, linguists and folklorists as a purely technical matter, for members of the indigenous community it can be a profound emotional issue deeply bound up with group identity and self-concept. Such ethnic attitudes toward literacy (both indigenous and colonial) play an important role in the editing and publishing of Aboriginal texts.[4] We also follow the standard conventions of English regarding punctuation and capitalization. In practice this is usually the last feature of the text to be confirmed, and requires close comparison of the grammar and style of the original and translation, so that the relationship of the clauses and sentences within the discourse is clear.

At some point early on, before the process goes too far, it is important to proofread. At this point, the transcriber and another editor go over the transcription line by line against the tape, and reach agreement on any problem areas such as ambiguous line turnings, false starts, etc. The dialogue is very important. Points of debate or dispute are also important and should be noted. The process of listening to the tape together can be very educational, especially when one of the team is a Native speaker of Tlingit or Haida, and the other is not. While some tapes and speakers are as clear as the proverbial bell, other tapes may be damaged or the speech unclear, so that the tape is virtually impossible for someone other than a Native speaker to understand. This reinforces the need for indigenous people to be involved in the documentation of their own oral traditions. It is much easier for a Native speaker to learn the professional and technical aspects of the linguistics and folklore involved than for a linguist or folklorist from outside to learn the language and cultural context.

At this point in the editing, most of our concern is with the line turnings and gross errors such as missing a line or phrase, but it should involve as much checking of spelling as possible. At some point, linguistic proofreading should be done with an outside specialist who can double-check the accuracy of the spelling. We have noted over the years a general resistance to proofreading by beginning transcribers, who are defensive of their work and see proofreading as 'finding fault' or 'picking it apart.' Our preference is to have mistakes and weaknesses spotted by friends and colleagues before the product stands up to the scrutiny of the entire world. On the other hand, we confess that the process of proofreading has brought us to the brink of divorce more often than any other element in our marriage.

When the line turnings are confirmed by proofreading against the tape, the lines should be numbered. We usually count by fives or tens. This provides a point of reference for the annotations. When translating, we have found it useful to number each sentence as an interim stage. As the editing continues, the translation becomes more fine-tuned, and aligned more accurately with the line turnings of the original text in a facing translation. The two languages will not match up line by line, but the sentences can and should match. We have found it difficult for beginning translators to distinguish simple from complex sentences, so that dependent clauses involving phrases beginning with 'when,' 'as,' 'while,' etc. are often mistranslated in first drafts, and gradually restored as the linguistic match-up becomes more precise.

In all of this, don't overlook the trivia, omission of which will eventually lead to grief later on: be sure to number the pages, date the draft manuscript and date all print-outs. It is helpful to keep all print-outs in case problems arise later on, but be sure to make corrections on the latest print-out. We have also noted a tendency of beginners to retranscribe, so that we may end up with two or three versions. Unless dated, these can create chaos. With both the Tlingit and Haida work, we now often find ourselves returning to drafts first done perhaps twenty years ago. In addition to making changes because of the increased skill developed by the transcriber in the intervening years, editing may also be required because of changes in spelling conventions. It is also important to identify on the transcription the name of the tradition-bearer, the recorder, and the date and place of the performance, as well as the name of the transcriber. Also, keep track of all computer files. It is very easy to get confused with duplicates and lose track of the 'latest, greatest' version. It's embarrassing to admire your work hot off the press only to discover that a semi-final computer file found its way into publication, and the one with corrections did not.

It is difficult to estimate the amount of time required to work with an oral text. One of our colleagues says, 'Every minute of tape takes one hundred minutes to sort out.' Another estimates eight hours of transcription for every hour of tape. A short narrative can easily take one day to transcribe, another to proof, another to translate, and two or three to type. So, it is not unreasonable to estimate a week of work for first, working drafts of the basic transcription and facing translation. This does not include the time for editing and proofreading of the transcription and the translation, and the match-up in facing translation format. Nor does this estimate include research for annotations, or into the biography of the tradition-bearer, to be discussed below. Given how difficult it is to find funding, to schedule work sessions with elders, and to cope with shifting personal and political dynamics of the community, it is easy to see how a short narrative can take twenty-five years to complete.

Equally important to understanding the time involved is appreciation of the energy and concentration required. We have found bureaucracies in general not appreciative of the time, stress, and skill required for doing this kind of work. One of our students was hired by a village heritage program, and difficulties arose over expectations. We tried to affirm to him and his employer that this kind of work requires intensive periods of focus without distraction or interruption, followed by periods of a break such as a run or walk around the block or something similar. It is impossible to do this work in a standard eight to five time frame in a noisy office. To push beyond a breaking time is to invite errors that will take even more time to sort out later. Furthermore, there is an emotional side of the work that we also need to keep in mind. The most difficult aspect for us is always working with death and dying, with seemingly endless grief. We are almost always working with the voices of the departed, or with elders probably in their last decade of life. Our message here is 'Be kind to your transcriber.' The job requires technical skills in Native language literacy, linguistics, and folklore, and also requires emotional skills to deal with stress and grief. It is unfortunate when office bureaucracies become insensitive to what it really takes to do the job. Treatment of staff can easily become inhumane when it becomes an exercise of political power. Unfortunately, such local, cultural, and personal considerations seem to be on the decline in the modern workplace, where the models of business and bureaucracy, both Native and non-Native, become increasingly 'hard-nosed.'

The final step in the first round of proofreading is to read the draft transcription back to the tradition-bearer whenever possible. We have always benefitted from this. The storyteller can usually clarify points that may be unclear to the transcriber. In some cases, the elder may wish to change something. For example, one storyteller requested that we delete a song that he included as part of his story. We agreed, and simply noted this in the annotations. This process guarantees that you end up with a text acceptable to the tradition-bearer. We can't emphasize enough the delight that most elders have felt at hearing their story read back to them. They know the text is in their own words and not a retelling or paraphrase. The late Tom Peters of Teslin commented, 'It's been years since I've heard a story like that!' This gave us pause to consider what it must be like to be the primary (or only) story teller in the community. Who tells you stories? Then he went on to suggest, 'Let me tell you the rest of it!'

Thus far, we've been talking about what we write and write about. It's equally important to say a few words about what not to write or talk about. Most folklorists eventually encounter the moral and ethical question of when to stop and what not to do. This can include publishing gossip or information that may be embarrassing or hurtful to the tradition-bearer, to others, or to the community. The problem may also involve dealing with culturally taboo subjects that may be perceived as spiritually and even physically harmful to individuals and the community. How folklorists grow in such understanding is powerfully shown by comparing Barre Toelken's seminal 'Yellowman' essay of 1969, reprinted in 1976, with an article he prepared eighteen years later (1987). There is nothing 'wrong' with the earlier article, but the later one describes levels of understanding that the author was not aware of as a younger scholar. He shows how a story may operate on several levels, and he concludes that it is appropriate not to discuss those levels which are taboo in the community, such as witchcraft. We encounter similar problems from time to time, and we have avoided publishing certain information, and even working with certain stories. In researching life stories, we have found that it is often necessary to ask subjects or their families if there are things they do not want included; otherwise, we run the risk of stumbling on the information or publishing it by mistake. This is a very serious level of editing that each scholar or collaborative team must eventually confront and resolve.

4 Translation into English

The next step in the process is to translate the transcribed text into English. Again, we begin with the endpoint. We prefer a facing, literary translation, with the Tlingit text on the left-hand page, and the English translation on the right. Another popular format is interlinear, either with a literal, word-for-word translation, or a literary translation, or both. Haida lends itself to a literal interlinear format more than Tlingit because Haida is more like English in its use of isolated words and free morphemes in reasonably similar order. In contrast, Tlingit has mostly bound morphemes in an order unlike English. Our current Haida project will feature the facing literary translation format, but will also include literal interlinear versions because of their linguistic value for students of the language. In some cases, we find a glossary helpful as a tool for students using the book to learn the language. We did this in our oratory book (1990), and in our narratives (1987) we analyzed interesting verbs in the annotations, although not all critics shared our enthusiasm for stunning examples of Tlingit grammar. The point is that the bilingual editions can be used for literature in translation and they can also be used as texts and models for learning the original language.

Now let us look at content rather than presentation. Libraries have been written on translation theory (see, for example, Voegelin 1954; Swann 1983, 1992, 1994). The main distinction we wish to emphasize here is between a translation and a paraphrase. Over the years, we have found the the Summer Institute of Linguistics/Wycliffe Bible Translators concepts of literal, minimal, and literary transfers to be most practical and useful (Nida 1964, 184–92). A literal transfer is word-for-word, even though it may not make sense in English; a minimal transfer is the bare minimum that makes sense in English, i.e., that meets the basic grammatical requirements of the target or receptor language, but without additional attention to style. The literary transfer stays as close as possible to the minimal transfer, but gives the translation more style and polish, with attention to the stylistic levels of the original, but ideally not lapsing over into paraphrase or embellishment. We won't go into any further theory here. Instead, we will mention some of the most interesting problems that keep recurring. The main point in all of this is that we are working from the transcribed text in Tlingit, attempting to make the English translation as close and as accurate as possible, but also with the basic requirement that it sound like English and make sense in English, with a level of style corresponding to the original – the 'texture' as described in Dundes (1964) and Toelken (1976). That's our goal. Oversimplified: 'text' is the 'story'; 'context' is the cultural setting; and 'texture' is the way in which the story is told – intonation, choice of vocabulary, gestures, etc. – everything that contributes to the 'meta-message' about how we are to understand the text. Is it humorous? Ironic? As a rule, the more important the textual features, the more difficult to translate. Looking at our old translations, we often find lapses into 'translation-ese' or unnatural stiffness, and we apologize for whatever shortcomings may appear over time as we – hopefully – get better at this.

We have observed that beginning translators often tend to use an inappropriate level of style in English. What is simple and direct in the original may be rendered with a 'higher' level of vocabulary, often stilted or cliché, so that damsels and fair maidens frequently appear. When elders play with levels of style or use various synonyms or euphemisms in the original, we try to reflect this in translation, choosing, for example, 'defecate' over other candidates in the verbal range only if that's the tone of the original.

The first draft of the English translation is done by the Native-language-speaking member of the editorial team. For Tlingit, this is Nora Marks Dauenhauer; for Haida, Charles Natkong, Sr. Then we argue about it. The argument usually consists of Richard Dauenhauer saying, 'It doesn't make sense!' and Nora Dauenhauer holding firm and saying 'Yes it does!' Who's right? We both are. It's not just a matter of the words, but of the syntax and discourse, the ordering of information within the sentence, and the connection of sentences within the larger unit (such as paragraph or section). We try to make the line and sentence our basic unit of translation, and we try to match the lines and sentences across the page in facing translation, but this is not always possible. The ordering of information in Tlingit is often the opposite of English, so that lines 1-2-3 in Tlingit commonly end up as 3-2-1 in English. We try not to rearrange the order of sentences in a larger context of discourse. But in relating sentences, we find translating conjunctions very frustrating, because the English and Tlingit ranges of meaning do not completely overlap. Thus, ḵu.aa may mean 'however,' but it may also introduce new information without implying a contrast. Another problem is the common word áwé, which means 'it is,' but which also functions as a phrase boundary marker, like a verbal comma. We try to translate it when it conveys lexical meaning, but not when it operates like a verbal comma (for more detail on these examples, see Dauenhauer and Dauenhauer 1987).

Another major source of confusion in translation is the Tlingit preference for pronouns over nouns.[5] One classic example is a Raven story that doesn't mention the noun 'Raven' until the very end. After all, it's obviously a Raven story! But what is obvious in the Tlingit oral context may not be obvious to younger non-Tlingit-speaking readers within the Tlingit community, or to readers beyond the community of origin. So, for clarity in translation, we change some of the pronouns to nouns where absolutely necessary. The trick is to make enough explicit in the English translation that the reader can follow the story with the same ease that a listener could follow it in the original. For most readers, the impact and power of the story will not come from the Tlingit or Haida original, but from the English translation. The hard thing for the translator is to accept the translation as the 'new original.' The original always haunts the translator, but for the English reader, the translation becomes now the original. We hope that the facing bilingual format will lead some readers back to savour some of the richness of the original language text, but in order to do this, the translation must have the power to stand on its own with clarity, power, and appeal.

We noted above that the phrase, line, and sentence are the basic units of translation. It is very important to recognize and make clear the relationship among the phrases within the sentence, and the sentences within the larger unit of discourse. We have found that beginning translators often have difficulty with this. Technically, it means identifying dependent and independent clauses, and handling transitions clearly. There is a difference, for example, between 'he goes' as a main verb, and 'if he goes,' or 'as he goes,' or 'when he goes,' in which cases the information is connected to additional information in the sentence. These are clearly marked morphemically in Tlingit and Haida, and need to be marked syntactically in English through conjunctions and punctuation.[6]

For our Haida work, we are encountering a dimension of difficulty in addition to the problems we find with Tlingit. At the age of sixty-seven, Mr Natkong is the youngest speaker of Haida in Alaska. He makes no claim to fluency, and is probably more of a passive bilingual, understanding far more than he speaks. He frequently finds himself not knowing some of the vocabulary or syntax of a story. In this case, he telephones among the few remaining speakers of Haida for help, often in vain. This is unfortunately the situation in which many of our colleagues working in other Native American languages find or will soon find themselves. As the number of fully fluent speakers of the oldest generations diminishes, the stylistic range of the younger generations of speakers becomes increasingly limited. The oral texts become important models for and records of the widest possible stylistic ranges of the tradition.

In our work with Haida folklore from Alaska, another interesting pattern is emerging. The forthcoming collection edited by Charles Natkong, Sr and Richard Dauenhauer features what are probably the last traditional stories told in Haida, in Alaska at least. This is a bold statement, and requires some explanation. We are working with texts recorded in Haida in the early 1970s from elders no longer alive. As we examine two recent published collections of Haida texts, we notice that virtually all of the traditional material is either re-elicited from Swanton's transcriptions recorded at the turn of the century, or told in English and back-translated into Haida. Enrico 1995 consists entirely of older material in Skidegate dialect collected by Swanton from September 1900 to August 1901 as part of the Jesup North Pacific Expedition; Enrico has carefully field-checked and confirmed the texts with the most knowledgeable speakers, and has published them in new transcription. He has a similar work in progress for Massett texts. In Eastman and Edwards (1991), the eleven stories are arranged in four groups: traditions, reminiscences, Western forms, and tales. The Western forms in the book are extremely interesting: a recipe for fried bread and a Haida version of Psalm 46, 'God Is With Us.' The editors describe the discourse patterns in detail, contrasting oral and written, and English and Haida discourse rules, showing how the oral fried bread recipe and psalm translation follow the storytelling patterns of traditional Haida narrative.

The current state of Haida oral literature is embodied in this book: the longest and most substantial texts (the two historical traditions and the three tales) are all re-elicited from earlier Haida texts, or translated from earlier English accounts, whereas the genres actually collected in performance were the reminiscences and the Western forms. Of these, the personal reminiscences (if one can be judgmental) are the skimpiest. The commentary is usually longer than the text. As far as I (Richard) can tell from my own field experience in Haida, this is the most popular folklore genre in Haida today. Most local publications as well as unpublished transcriptions and translations with which I am familiar include many such reminiscences, and a majority of them describe idealized childhood and hypothetical history. Although the editors do not draw the conclusion explicitly, it is clear from the range of texts included and from the editors' valuable notes that reminiscences and Western forms are more viable in Haida folklore and folklife today than traditional histories and tales. In other words, we seem to have reached the point of diminishing returns regarding 'traditional genres,' and, although there will be some kind of group dynamics and attitudes surrounding these genres, we probably should look elsewhere for viable folklore genres, such as among the recipes and psalms. From the folklore point of view, these Western forms are interesting because, like reminiscences, they may be collected abundantly in performance, unlike traditional genres (such as history and Raven stories) which are clearly on their way out. A shared, 'national' or 'tribal' oral literature may no longer exist for Haida, at least in the Haida language, and even possibly in English, whereas the more individual, personal and family memorates and Western forms are strong. Eastman and Edwards make a valuable contribution to folklore method because, without the description of how the editors actually obtained the Haida versions, we would have only the texts, and even with the other valuable notes on the cultural context and meaning of the stories, we would have no sense of the relative viability of the genres. But, in addition to providing valuable Haida texts, this rather thin volume confirms the experience of other fieldworkers. Usually we get such confirmation only over beer or coffee at professional meetings. In the context of our present paper, this is an example of a dimension of editing that we can expect to encounter more frequently in the future, and a dimension very important to consider.

5 Annotation

As we have already noted, oral performance tends to be highly contextualized in its most natural settings. Vocabulary, syntax, discourse, and content combine in the original and even more so in translation to create a laconic and confusing text. We deal with this in what we have called 'the ubiquitous footnote.' About the same time as the translation and proofreading are underway, the process of annotation begins. Once the lines are numbered, problem areas can be identified and explained in notes.

For the original oral audience, the linguistic and cultural peers of the tradition-bearer, much knowledge was assumed and shared. For audiences of another language, culture, or generation, problems of understanding arise when the basic information and assumptions are no longer shared. Putting any literary text into cultural context is a problem that folklorists and literary scholars have addressed for years. Our favourite example for English is the opening of *Richard III*, 'Now is the winter of our discontent made glorious summer by this sun of York.' These lines make no sense at all without some appreciation of English climate, history, and political symbolism, and how they are poetically charged by simile and metaphor.

What requires annotation should be worked out by the editorial team. Place names is a topic we have encountered. Northwest-coast oral literature tends to be highly localized. The personal and place names are important, and typically relate to historical or spiritual covenants with clan ancestors. George Vancouver happily named the places he encountered on this coast for his patrons in the British Admiralty and Royal Family. Needless to say, the places are contextualized differently in local oral tradition. In the stories, the first reaction of an outsider might be, 'Is this a real place?' Annotations can fill in the information implied but not explicitly stated by the narrator, but known to his or her peers. A good example among our new Haida texts is a biographical narrative that never mentions the name of the subject. Again the outsider's question: 'Is this a real story?' And the insider's reply: 'Sure. It's Samuel G. Davis' – along with the puzzled look that adds, 'Everybody knows that!' As a rule of thumb, if a pattern begins to appear in the notes, it is probably worth devoting a paragraph or section to that topic or concept in the preface or introduction.

Northwest-coast oral literature is inseparable from social structure and the crest designs owned by the various clans. This especially requires annotation, much the same as notes to *Richard III* might explain the roses of Lancaster and York. Likewise notes and introductory essays can explain an underlying world view that might not be clear to readers. Our notes to the Hoonah speeches from 1968 and the Sitka speeches from 1980 vary in level of detail (Dauenhauer and Dauenhauer 1990); in the earlier speeches the traditional world view is still intact, but in the later ones the elders are aware that a generation gap has opened, and they begin to make things more explicit that were earlier only implied.

The trick with notes and introductions is not to ruin the story for the reader, but to clarify points assumed by the narrator that might be missed or misunderstood by someone outside the tradition. One example is where editors have 'cleaned up' the stories. In one popular story, a girl steps in bear scat and verbally abuses the bear. This violates a cultural taboo against speaking or even thinking disrespectfully about animals, and sets the entire sequence of events into action. By deleting the reference to excrement, the editors have deleted the entire reason for the existence and power of the story. Some educators have advised against including unpleasant elements such as death. This is like the Easter story without the Crucifixion.[7]

If traditional stories are transcribed and translated correctly, they will raise as many questions as they answer. The questions of substance remain eternal and answerable only as each reader engages with the story; that's why the stories are eternal and powerful. But questions of cultural context can be addressed in notes and essays. We need to expect the stories to be culturally different. Unfortunately, all of us tend to like and understand what's familiar. We should note here that the only negative review of our *Haa kusteeyí* (1994) came from a librarian in Vancouver who didn't like the stories because Tlingit literature isn't what she's used to from her background in European fairy tales and children's literature. She writes, 'For those of us raised with stories whose purpose was most commonly to instil the moral values of our own culture, these tales require an enormous amount of work to determine why they are being told and what, if any, point they are making' (Mason 1987). She didn't like the Tlingit stories only because they weren't European. But that's the point.

6 Reactions

The study of reactions by various audiences to a text transcribed from oral tradition and now on the printed page in bilingual format with the original text and facing English translation moves us away from the technical aspects of applied linguistics to the domain and dimensions of sociolinguistics. Reaction to books like those we produce includes both views of literacy from traditionally non-literate people, and views of oral literature from members of the long-literate Western tradition. The overwhelming reaction to our books by readers and reviewers has been positive. Our books have been favourably reviewed in over two dozen journals and newspapers reflecting both professional and popular assessments. But, with apologies to Tolstoy, all good reactions and reviews are alike; each negative reaction is negative in its own way. This makes them more interesting to talk about.

Most readers of various cultures responded positively to the visual presentation of the texts on the printed page. But the most puzzling thing about the page for some white or highly acculturated Tlingit readers was the short line format. Poetry has short lines and a ragged right margin, and prose is rectangular with a flush right margin; therefore these can't be stories but have to be poems. This seemingly trivial issue presented insurmountable barriers for some readers. A far more serious and pervasive problem is the prejudice against oral literature that seems to prevail generally in schools and universities. We have observed this ourselves and we receive ongoing reports from colleagues. The prejudice is manifested in the reluctance of the educational establishment to accept contemporary oral literature as serious, adult literature, despite the overwhelming acceptance of oral literature of the past such as Gilgamesh, the Bible, Homer, and *Beowulf* into the academic canon. It is often difficult to communicate to conventional English departments a 'vision of literature as a concept that encompasses oral as well as written traditions' (Lord 1995, ix). Indigenous literature, whether oral or written, is still struggling for full inclusion in the canon (Krupat 1989). Native American oral literature is generally trivialized or relegated to the category of children's literature. This is not to suggest that there are no children's stories to be found in Native oral literature, but that generic treatment of non-White literature as children's literature is racist and that this widespread attitude deserves re-examination (see Johnston 1991, 13).

In the course of his writings, A.B. Lord continually rose to the defense of oral literature, in the face of ongoing prejudice against it from a literary (and literate) 'establishment' that tends to deny, minimalize, or misunderstand oral poetics both ancient and contemporary. Lord repeatedly emphasized the importance of oral-traditional literature in Western heritage and culture (see especially 1991, chaps. 1 and 2). We should note here that Lord's main concepts apply to North American indigenous oral traditions as well, the obvious difference being that there is no Native American epic narrative singing tradition characterized by metrical composition. In contrast, as far as we know, indigenous North American narratives and oratory are 'prose.' With this modification of Lord's theory, his concepts of theme and formula also apply to North American Aboriginal traditions.[8]

One remedy that we encourage is the offering of more courses in oral literature that would utilize the rich and growing body of ethnopoetic work over the last twenty-five years. Such courses should include the classics of Western and non-Western oral tradition, as well as contemporary oral texts. Such courses would result in wider appreciation for the stylistic and compositional aesthetics of oral literature as a genre, and set the background for highlighting specific cultural traditions of special interest. We encourage weekend community retreats as one format for such courses. Whether in a conventional course or community weekend retreat, our approach is conservative and text-based, as old as Socratic dialogue. We read the text together as a group, and talk about it. What did we notice about it? Our motive is to show that the 'old stories' are not antiquarian, trivial, irrelevant, or marginal, but are important for today. We see Aboriginal literature as serious, adult material. It's not children's literature. Young adults in Native communities in North American have unprecedented opportunities their parents and grandparents never had; but they also have unprecedented problems and temptations as well, in the form of drugs and AIDS in addition to alchohol. We see Aboriginal oral literature as one way of addressing these community issues. As the title of the PBS series with Joseph Campbell and Bill Moyers (1988) suggests, this is 'the power of myth.' The new buzzwords are 'self esteem' and 'self-concept.' The old, Socratic buzzword is 'know thyself.' Without a specific text to anchor it, discussion of 'the culture' can become quite vague. The stories are repositories of specific knowlege and data, and examples of cultural values and wisdom in action. The stories are a great place to begin. Our goal as editors is to end up with a published text. Our goal as readers and teachers is to begin with such a text.

Whereas people socialized into highly literate traditions tend to be puzzled or suspicious of oral tradition, members of traditions without widespread popular indigenous language literacy tend to be equally confused by and suspicious of the printed page. Probably the greatest anxiety is loss of control over the traditional oral relationship in 'real time' between the composer/performer and the audience.[9] This is a profound dimension and needs to be dealt with individually and patiently over time. Reaction to literacy is also a generational phenomenon, so that acceptance is more widely found among the youngest members of the community, and resistance among the older generations. As noted above, non-literacy is a powerful emblem of Native ethnicity for many people, and to the extent that literacy as a concept is identified with colonial and non-indigenous languages and cultures, even literacy in the indigenous language may be resisted for emotional and political reasons.

An extension of the confusion over literacy is the sense that something is being stolen. The concept of clan ownership of oral material as well as emblems is strong and widespread on the Northwest coast. In most cases, the material is not secret or esoteric, but rights to transmit are restricted to members of the owning clan who are recognized as masters of the tradition by their peers. To address this anxiety, we include several features in our publications. As noted above, we feature prominently the name and genealogy of the tradition-bearer, and we always include as part of the text whatever narrative frame is included in the oral performance. Beyond this, we feature biographies of varying lengths in our books. We did this tentatively in our first collection (1987). The positive reaction from readers and critics was so overwhelming that we 'went overboard' and had to restrict the biographies to a two-page sketch with one photograph in our second book (1990), but we expanded the concept to a nine hundred page life history volume (1994). Whenever we do readings, we begin with a guided tour of the book: the introduction, the facing texts, the notes, and the biographies. Our position is that we are not retelling another person's story without authorization, but we are an amplification in time and space of a single performance by a specific tradition-bearer. We show the photograph, and tell about the elder, and ask our audience to consider us as an extension of the storyteller whose work we are reading. Reaction to our featuring the elders has been positive.

All of this is to make several points: that folklore is not anonymous, but is shaped and reshaped by specific individuals; and that we are not telling their stories, but are presenting their performances. The nagging question of money often comes up, and we state that we are salaried to document the material, but that we receive no royalties or returns from the material itself. Returns go to meet the costs of printing, and royalties go to the Sealaska Heritage Foundation.

Still, the problem of ownership remains. Who owns the stories? This is a difficult question, easily wrapped up in political correctness and cliché. In Tlingit, the stories are the property of the clan. But for each instance, there is a specific telling by a specific elder. Most often, state, federal, and private funds have been involved. Often several institutions and individuals have collaborated. Our own work began over twenty-five years ago. It started on our own and grew in creative partnership with many institutions, most recently, with Sealaska Heritage Foundation, a non-profit 501(c)3 affiliate of Sealaska Corporation, one of the 'Native Corporations' created under the Alaska Native Claims Settlement Act of 1971. As editors, we make no claims to ownership of the material.

The most enthusiastic response to our work is coming from the young adults of high school age through their thirties and forties. Thus, the greatest appreciation of printed versions of oral literature is from the generations least involved in oral tradition. We sense that they appreciate their situation: they are raised within the Tlingit community, but not within the traditional language, culture, and oral tradition. They know that they are not getting it any other way but from books; they are not getting the language and oral traditions directly from parents or grandparents due to the many wedges that have been driven into the process of natural transmission by historical and social developments of the last hundred years.

For the last generation of traditionally raised elders, our work is largely irrelevant. Most of them still operate within the language and oral tradition. For the members of this generation who choose to work with us, the printed page becomes a vehicle for transcendence of the oral literature beyond their immediate lifetime. Some members of this generation decline to have their material recorded and published out of fear that it will be abused or desecrated; but others are concerned that the stories and models survive. The ideal vehicle for survival is stewardship and natural transmission within the community, but this is no longer possible in many places in the indigenous language, although it may be possible in English (Kwachka 1992). It's the difference between the salmon run and smoked fish; the berry patch and jars of jam.

The most varied reaction to our work comes from the middle generation, those aged roughly between forty-five and seventy-five. Depending on their family circumstances, these people were raised in the oral tradition to some degree, speak the language to some degree, yet are also involved in English language schooling and employment in the cash economy. This generation is characteristically most involved in tribal politics, having come of age during the struggle for land claims, and during the now twenty-five years of the corporate structure established in 1971 by passage of the Alaska Native Claims Settlement Act (ANCSA). In ways that we cannot begin to analyze here, ANCSA has restructured Alaska Native life, impacting social structure, leadership, political discourse, and worldview. In many cases, organizational development and management style are modelled after multinational corporations such as Exxon and others. We question the wisdom and practicality of applying such models. There is (or should be) an instrinsic difference between a large, multinational corporation with political or cultural allegiance to no community or nation in particular, and a local Native American profit or non-profit corporation that operates within traditional contexts of family, clan, kinship, and community. At the corporate level, the work of cultural documentation and preservation is often and unfortunately viewed in terms of political strategy or profit, with expectations that the programs will turn a profit for the corporation and result in votes from the shareholders for individuals on the board of directors.

We don't want to create a straw man (or straw person) here, but it is important in the context of this work to voice concern over an emerging pattern in the Tlingit and Haida communities and probably in other indigenous communities in the United States and Canada as well: political correctness. We hope this development will be short-lived, although such hopes are unrealistic. Politicization of cultural issues is nothing new, but the new political correctness has interesting dimensions. We are concerned about the connection between political correctness and neo-positivism. We find ourselves, along with some colleagues of our generation, bewildered by the neo-positivism of political correctness among the younger generation, when our generation was raised to question positivism. It seems that one generation fights positivism and the next embraces it. Scholars have been fighting Nazism, communism, and religious dogma for a century, only to see kindred forms of positivism and political correctness arise in the profession.

For example, one member of the controlling board of an Alaska Native foundation was adamant that the work of the organization 'not benefit white people.' In our view this attitude is simplistic, unrealistic, and short-sighted, not to mention racist. Many members of the board are of mixed ancestry. The children of this particular board member are of mixed ancestry (although non-white). We certainly oppose the exploitation of indigenous cultural material by outsiders, but the material is not secret or esoteric, and it seems reasonable to most people that the oral literature should be presented in accurate and sensitive ways to the interested, intelligent readers regardless of ethnic background. Non-Russians can be enriched by Tolstoy; white Americans can learn from Achebe.

Political correctness extends to areas many scholars consider reasonably neutral. At a recent conference, the male co-author of this paper was attacked by two feminists for being a sexist colonialist. He was told that it is sexist to translate 'he/she/it' in the target language (English) when the source language (Tlingit) does not distinguish gender. As writers, scholars, and translators, we consider ourselves sensitive to issues of gender, but it is difficult to know which options really exist. This is not the same as the perennial problem with grammatical gender in Greek, Latin, and Hebrew, or attempts to create gender-neutral English translations of scripture where theologically appropriate. Our male co-author didn't bother to rebut the feminists with the observation that Tlingit doesn't even mark the third person pronoun at all; it's zero. Does this mean that we should just zero out all the female gender references in English translation? Then the translation is no longer English. We recognize the theoretical problem, but it seems to be of the same nature as Tlingit being marked differently than English for aspect and tense; does this mean that we omit tense in English translation because Tlingit doesn't have it? It is impossible. The translator must act as an editor and select from the range of English possibilities the choice that best expresses and corresponds to the original; to copy is impossible. It seems reasonable to use feminine pronouns in English where women are referred to in Tlingit.

On this occasion, Richard was also accused of being colonial. 'It's colonial to annotate Aboriginal texts with an "outside" reader in mind. Let the outsider learn,' he was told. This accusation applies to the method to which we both subscribe. It was interesting that, judging from her accent, the woman was of German ancestry. She had learned English and was presumably working with a Canadian First Nations language and oral tradition. Richard smiled and didn't offer a 'yes, but' at the time. But it does seem very provincial and very simplistic to assume that any outsider, regardless of enthusiasm and skill, can learn all the nuances of every other culture on earth. It's taking Richard, the newcomer, one lifetime to find out what little he feels he knows about Tlingit. Who has enough lifetimes to do this for all the other oral literary traditions that we would enjoy reading in translation? We appreciate annotations and explanations to help those such as ourselves who are trying to learn and appreciate other indigenous traditions. We hope that those not familiar with Tlingit will appreciate our annotations. It is very important to note that this group of learners is not limited to outsiders, but also includes younger generations of the ethnic group that were not raised in the language and traditional culture. It seems to us that the only alternative to annotations is ignorance. The attitude that 'Us people of colour mystically understand all other people of colour' may be politically correct, but it's also naïve.

Problems of translation and annotation are undeniable and complex. Needless to say, when these particular feminists do their own translations, they can do them any way they like. But in our opinion, it offers no help to confuse the real issues of translation, documentation, and editing with layers of political correctness.[10]

Among Tlingit people, we have many enthusiastic supporters in the forty-five to seventy-five age group; but we also have many detractors. Some of the reaction is human weakness, especially jealousy and suspicion of great personal wealth being accumulated from commercial exploitation of stories – 'getting rich off the culture.' For those who can speak the language, denial of literacy is important as a badge of Native ethnicity and the language is often used as a social statement rather than for serious communication. For those who do not speak the language, the language often serves as a reminder of things they fear or do not know, contributing to a sense of guilt, inferiority, or hostility. This is a serious emotional wound that will take time and care to heal. This generation also seems to be in greatest denial of the extreme danger of language extinction, and seems to hold unrealistic expectations for the survival of the language. Members of this generation by and large hold a simplistic view of the complexity of the language and culture which we call the 'genetic fallacy' – that the language will magically survive with little or no effort on the basis of ethnicity alone (Dauenhauer and Dauenhauer 1997).

The reaction to our books is often, 'That's easy. I can do that, too,' or 'I know that story too,' or 'They just put it in a book.' The general resistance to indigenous literacy in this generation raises emotional barriers for many individuals that prevent them from admitting the need for training in literacy, folklore, and applied linguistics that would contribute to their success. There is a general lack of understanding or appreciation of the time, energy, training, and expense that go into publication. This perception is magnified with an exaggerated image of financial profits derived from academic publishing. Transcribing and translating oral literature is not everybody's cup of tea. The work requires a certain personality. It can be tedious, exacting, and emotionally intense. It requires and instills a certain humility in the face of the Great Tradition. All of this is difficult or impossible to understand for persons who view themselves as the source of all knowledge and tradition, as some individuals in this generation unfortunately do.

The most interesting aspect of the behaviour of this generation is their view of the culture as alienable, something that one puts on and takes off at will (Dauenhauer and Dauenhauer 1995). Considering the political environment of this generation's coming of age, it is not surprising to find 'the culture' increasingly politicized and politically exploited. Any aspect of 'the culture' can easily become a token in a personal or group struggle for power and control in community or regional politics. Archives into which elders deposited stories to be transcribed and published can be closed. Programs can be strangled and destroyed. People can also be destroyed.

This 'dark side' is a powerful control. There is a Japanese proverb, 'The nail that sticks up, gets hammered down.' There are Native writers of great talent working quietly in communities. But for some reason (and we think it's fear of being hammered down) they are reluctant to share their work beyond their own classroom or immediate community. We support the concept of locally produced materials, but we regret, with so few workers in the field, that good work cannot be shared more widely. The ultimate tragedy of this middle generation is that its members have the potential to cultivate or to destroy. Among its members are the last on earth who speak the language well enough to be able to join the effort to document and teach it. But to do this, each individual of such talent and potential must first do battle with the overwhelming emotional and social forces that impact this generation in ways that no other generation of Tlingit or Haida people has suffered before.

Part of the problem is that the language and community situations have changed radically, and the customs of traditional usage have become confused. A hundred years ago, the community would have been more monolithic and monolingual in Tlingit. Race, language, and culture were largely congruent. There were few 'outsiders' to worry about. Now it is ethnically mixed and English is the dominant language of the Tlingit people. Now the 'insiders' are in a minority and are acutely aware of this. This also heightens the sense of ownership. The sense of possession applies not only to publication of oral literature and other 'intellectual property,' but to the study of language as well. Whites have been accused of 'stealing the language.' Part of the emotional confusion that individuals and communities must resolve is the increasing sense of possession now combined with the increasing awareness of loss, not from theft from without, but through lack of transmission within.

Most often, 'We'll do it ourselves' results in nothing being done at all, which satisfies the desire for secrecy, but thwarts transmission to the next generation. Often relatives or descendants of elders in the 'middle generation' are more protective than the elders themselves. Elders may request that their oral material be recorded for future generations, but family, clan members, or community bureaucracies may disagree for various reasons. There have been cases where one relative sabotaged an elder's attempts to have an event videotaped. There have been situations where children interfered with recording sessions, with the result that after the death of the parent, there was no record of what he knew and wanted to preserve for them. Only with the death of the elder did the younger people realize the enormity of their loss. They assumed that 'somebody' knew the 'the stories,' but this was not so. There are also cases in which elders taped stories, but the archives have become part of community bureaucracy and tribal politics, something to fight over, a perverse shrine to be venerated rhetorically but not touched or used, rather than understood as cultural heritage material to be transmitted to the next generation. In one community, access has been routinely denied to Native and non-Native scholars working together in an attempt to produce written instructional and cultural resource materials from the oral tapes. In one extreme example, we observed public rhetorical grandstanding in which one political leader demanded books based on the tapes, yet in private board meetings voted to deny access to the people she demanded do the transcription! Unless such tapes are worked with, they may soon deteriorate and fade. Some of the Natkong Haida tapes have begun to deteriorate, with 'bleed-through' that makes them extremely difficult for a Native-speaking linguist to transcribe and virtually unintelligible to an outsider. More tragically, there is a real danger with some languages (such as Haida) that even if the tapes survive, there will soon be nobody left alive who can understand what is on them. The tragedy here is that coming generations of that ethnic group will be left with neither the berry patch nor the jam. This is an extreme case of linguistic and cultural suicide.

In this line of work, we think often about the death of language. When any elder of any culture dies, the survivors experience a sense of cultural as well as personal loss. There are many levels of loss: personal, family, generational, local, regional, national, cultural, and linguistic. Working in the late 1990s with material recorded in the early 1970s, we sense that all of these levels are at risk. When an eighty- or ninety-year-old German-American or Scotch-Canadian elder dies, we lose the personal, family, generational, and local knowledge that such elders experienced. But in the case of Haida, with an estimated eighty speakers remaining, the loss extends to the entire nation, culture, and language. English and German are not in danger; the national histories of England, Scotland, Germany, and the United States are well documented, and the entire traditional culture will not be lost through the death of a single individual. But this is a danger with smaller indigenous languages and cultures around the world.

We appreciate the fear of desecration, but we believe that the risks of sharing information are less dangerous than the risk that it may otherwise be lost forever. We have seen audiences around the world be moved by stories and oratory whose original audiences were a single room. One of the Psalm verses sung by the choir and congregation in the Orthodox Church prior to the public reading of the Bible on Pentecost and at other times during the year is 'Their proclamation has gone out into all the earth, and their words to the end of the universe' (Ps. 19:4). We think of this often when we think of the tradition-bearers with whom we have worked. Through the books we have edited, it is not our words that go out, but the words of the great storytellers and orators of Tlingit tradition. Their words continue to inspire and delight, and be models for the continuation and development of the tradition. The Psalm verse is part of a larger description of the heavens, the skies, and the sun. We believe that verbal artists of the past are indeed luminaries for subsequent generations, and that their words were not meant to be kept in secret and quibbled over, but to be shouted out in joy. This verse is also quoted in Romans 10:18 in development of the theme that 'faith comes by hearing.' It is no distortion of that passage to say in the context of this paper that faith in self and tradition come by hearing the classics of that spiritual tradition, whatever it is. There is a discussion in Bettelheim (1976 [26–27]) of the Lewis Carroll poem in which Carroll calls a fairy tale a 'love-gift' to a child, a gift across the generations from an older person who is 'half a life asunder.' The Tlingit and Haida tradition-bearers with whose material we are now working gave fully and freely of their stories, as gifts of love to future generations, not as something to become a political battleground or to be claimed as spoils of greed or infighting.

7 Why do it?

So why do it, especially when it can hurt so much? We guess it's because it feels so good when it isn't hurting. We are as much energized by the enthusiasm of the young as we are discouraged by the middle-aged confused. But most of all, the balance is tipped by the value we place on the gems of oral tradition we have received from the elders. Contrary to popular opinion, we don't get rich on this. When we're lucky, we get salaried to transcribe and translate, or we get an honorarium to talk about it. But the rewards are spiritual, and the motivation must be spiritual as well.

There is a phrase we like by the poet Robinson Jeffers: 'The honey of peace in old poems.' We find this honey of peace in Homer and Gilgamesh, in the love poems of Sappho and the Greek Anthology. Because someone wrote them down, and the fragments of writing survive, the poems are alive today. The Russian poet Boris Pasternak refers to the poet as 'a hostage of eternity, a prisoner of time.' The poet is of and from eternity, held captive for the moment by time. The orators and storytellers of Native American oral tradition are poets and hostages as well, craftsmen and creators. We view the text as a vehicle of release to all eternity. We believe that in the final analysis, the Muse will still be found in control of poetry. 'Sing in me, Muse, and through me tell the story,' opens Fitzgerald's translation of Homer's *Odyssey*. We often feel like that, working with a text from oral tradition.

As we have emphasized before, there is no substitute for living oral tradition. Any printed page at best is a replica and substitute. But oral tradition is dying all around the world, even where the languages are viable, as in the case of the Russian and Serbian epic. Oral literature seems to be able to live well alongside literacy, but it has trouble surviving where post-literacy thrives in the form of radio, television, and videotapes. The situation is made extreme where the languages themselves are moribund, such as Haida and Tlingit.

To what extent the pattern of language loss can be reversed and the languages restored is unknown (Dauenhauer and Dauenhauer 1998). But in the field of documention, the effort of a single person can make a difference (R. Dauenhauer 1994b). Compare the situation of Mandarin Chinese, with an estimated seven hundred million speakers, to that of Eyak, with one speaker left. Nothing that any one of us does will impact the survival of Chinese or contribute significantly to documenting it. But we can make a difference in working with indigenous languages in many parts of the world. Those of us who do it, do it for satisfaction, because it feels good.

Within a few verses of each other in the Gospel of St. Matthew are two passages that helped us frame this section of the paper: 'Every scribe instructed concerning the kingdom of heaven is like a householder who brings out his treasure things new and old,' and 'A prophet is not without honor except in his own country' (Matt. 13:52, 57). We can identify with both passages, and we suspect that our colleagues will identify with them as well. Verse 52 is very Northwest-coast-like, calling to mind the clan house leader bringing crest art out of a bentwood box for ceremonial display, an image often used in oral literature of the region (Dauenhauer and Dauenhauer 1990, 313–15). This is the way it feels to work with oral literature. The scribe is compared to the house leader, bringing out treasures for display or possibly distribution. Having experienced the vision or awareness of the beauty and power of a performance of oral literature, the scribe works to present it in writing and transmit it on the printed page. As noted above, the effort is met with varying emotional reactions, and often 'A prophet is ... without honor ... in his own country.'

The risk of negative reaction is part of the job description. We should clarify that not all people want their voice to go out to all the world. This is a serious consideration, and we respect it when it is the legitimate desire of the tradition-bearer. But this raises another dimension of the question 'who is it for?' The file cabinet? Family, local, or clan distribution? Larger distribution? Our personal philosophy is that we no longer have the time and energy, much less the funding, to transcribe and translate secret documents for archives. We work only with situations in which people are committed to wider, permanent distribution within the context of cultural tradition, such as respect for clan ownership, recognition of the storytellers, concern for the style and language of the original performance. We think the risk is worth taking and the energy well spent when there is commitment by all involved for the words of the clan ancestors to go out to the end of the universe.

NOTES

1   We direct readers to several excellent books on folklore research and fieldwork in general, including Brunvand (1976, 1978); Dorson (1972); Goldstein (1964); Jackson (1987); and Toelken (1979). These works, new and old, offer sound advice on different aspects of fieldwork, from establishing rapport, setting tradition-bearers at ease, and conducting interviews, to technical problems of how to operate recording equipment, and legal and ethical problems such as payment and copyright.

2   The papers in the present volume by Cruikshank and Chamberlin also offer new insights, and evidence that the meaning of a cultural performance lies as much in the telling as in the text; i.e., that not only is the text not fixed in oral tradition, but the meaning of the text is not

fixed either, but emerges in practice. This is the difference between what a story 'says' and what a story 'does.' See also Cruikshank (1995a, 28, 34–6; 1995b, 70).

3 Examples of theory and practice may be found in Hymes (1981, 1987, 1989); Mattina (1989); Ramsey (1983); Rothenberg and Rothenberg (1983); Sherzer and Woodbury (1987); Swann (1983, 1987, 1992, 1994); and Swann and Krupat (1987).

4 For a fuller treatment, see Basso (1989); Dauenhauer and Dauenhauer (1998); Ong (1982); Saville-Troike (1989); Scollon and Scollon (1981); Scribner and Cole (1978); Tannen (1982); and Watahomigie and Yama-moto (1992).

5 The same situation has been noted for Koyukon (Attla 1989, 7; 1990, x) and Hupa (Bennett 1996) oral literature, and probably in many others.

6 As an aside here, this feature of language also applies to ESL and English composition. For example, Yup'ik Eskimo marks the main verb in a passage (or story!) for person, tense, and number. Other verbs have a generic ending meaning something like 'same as the above.' This can be rendered in English with '-ing,' but this often leads to strings of dangling participles in translation and freshman composition. Use of participles is also a main feature of Buriat-Mongol epic style, that translates something like 'verbing, verbing, verbing, and having verbed, he verbed.' Many of the topics mentioned above for Tlingit have also been addressed by colleagues working on Alaskan Athabaskan; see the introductions to Jones (1979) and Attla (1983, 1989, and 1990).

7 See Bettelheim 1976 for the psychological necessity of working through troubling elements in stories, and Sarris (1993) regarding problems of editing community texts for schools, and teaching indige-nous literature in the context of 'classroom culture.'

8 For a full discussion of this in the context of other studies (especially Foster 1974) see Dauenhauer and Dauenhauer (1990), 137–46.

9 The concepts and dynamics of audience have been described from various perspectives: see Cruikshank (1995b); Ong (1975); Scollon and Scollon (1979, 1981, 1995); Toelken (1976, 1987).

10 For more on the impact of political correctness on scholarship and public discourse, see Tannen (1998)

WORKS CITED

Attla, Catherine. 1983. *Sitsiy Yugh Noholnik Ts'in'/As My Grandfather Told It: Traditional Stories from the Koyukuk.* Told by Catherine Attla; transcribed by Eliza Jones; translated by Eliza Jones and Melissa Axelrod; illustrated by Cindy Davis. Nenana and Fairbanks: Yukon-Koyukuk School District and Alaska Native Language Center.

–. 1989. *Bakk'aatugh Ts'uhuniy/Stories We Live By: Traditional Koyukon Athabaskan Stories told by Catherine Attla*. Transcribed by Eliza Jones; translated by Eliza Jones and Chad Thompson; illustrated by Cindy Davis. Nenana and Fairbanks: Yukon-Koyukuk School District and Alaska Native Language Center.

–. 1990. *K'etetaalkkaanee/The One Who Paddled Among the People and Animals: The Story of an Ancient Traveler*. Told by Catherine Attla; transcribed and translated by Eliza Jones; illustrated by Cindy Davis. Nenana and Fairbanks: Yukon-Koyukuk School District and Alaska Native Language Center.

Bailey, James. 1995. 'On Analyzing the Verbal Rhythm of a Russian Lyric Folk Song.' *Poetics Today* 16, no. 3: 471–91.

Bauman, Richard, and Joel Sherzer. 1989. *Explorations in the Ethnography of Speaking*. Second edition. Cambridge: Cambridge University Press.

Bennett, Ruth. 1996. Personal communication, and working draft of Chapter 2, *He Was Dug Up: A Guide to Understanding*, Humboldt State University, Center for Indian Community Development, forthcoming.

Bettelheim, Bruno. 1976. *The Uses of Enchantment: The Meaning and Importance of Fairy Tales*. New York: Knopf.

Blaeser, Kimberly M. 1994. *Trailing You*. Greenfield Center, New York: Greenfield Review Press.

Brunvand, Jan Harold. 1976. *Folklore: A Study and Research Guide*. New York: St. Martin's.

–. 1978. *The Study of American Folklore, An Introduction*. 2nd edition. New York: Norton.

Campbell, Joseph, and Bill Moyers. 1988. *Joseph Campbell and The Power of Myth, with Bill Moyers*. New York: Mystic Fire Video.

Campbell, Maria. 1995. *Stories of the Road Allowance People*. Penticton, British Columbia: Theytus Books.

Craig, Colette G. 1992. 'Language Shift and Language Death: The Case of Rama in Nicaragua.' *International Journal of the Sociology of Language* 93: 11–26.

Cruikshank, Julie. 1995a. 'Imperfect Translations: Rethinking Objects of Ethnographic Collection.' *Museum Anthropology* 19, no. 1: 25–38.

Cruikshank, Julie, in collaboration with Angela Sidney. 1995b. '"Pete's Song": Establishing Meanings through Story and Song.' In *When Our Words Return: Writing, Hearing, and Remembering Oral Traditions of*

Alaska and the Yukon, edited by Phyllis Morrow and William Schneider. Logan: Utah State University Press.

Dauenhauer, Nora Marks. 1988. *The Droning Shaman*. Haines, Alaska: Black Current Press.

—. 1991. 'Raven, King Salmon, and the Birds: A Play.' In *Raven Tells Stories: An Anthology of Alaskan Native Writing*, edited by Joseph Bruchac. Greenfield Center, New York: Greenfield Review Press.

Dauenhauer, Nora Marks, and Richard Dauenhauer. 1987. *Haa shuká / Our Ancestors: Tlingit oral narratives*. Seattle: University of Washington Press.

—. 1990. *Haa tuwunáagu yís / For Healing Our Spirit: Tlingit oratory*. Seattle: University of Washington Press.

—. 1992. 'Native language survival.' *Left Bank* 2 ('Extinction,' Special Issue, edited by Linny Stovall): 115–22.

—. 1994. *Haa kusteeyí / Our Culture: Tlingit life stories*. Seattle: University of Washington Press.

—. 1995. 'Oral literature embodied and disembodied.' In *Aspects of Oral Communication*, edited by Uta M. Quasthoff, 91–111. Berlin: De Gruyter.

—. 1997. 'Boas, Shotridge, and Indigenous Tlingit Ethnography.' Paper presented at the Jesup Centenary Conference, American Museum of Natural History, New York, November 1997.

—. 1998. 'Technical, Emotional, and Ideological Issues in Reversing Language Shift: Examples from Southeast Alaska.' In *Endangered Languages: Language Loss and Community Response*, edited by Lenore Grenoble and Lindsay Whaley, 57–98. Cambridge: Cambridge University Press.

Dauenhauer, Richard. 1975. 'Text and Context of Tlingit Oral Tradition.' PhD diss., University of Wisconsin, Madison.

—. 1976. 'The Narrative Frame: Style and Personality in Tlingit Prose Narrative.' *The Folklore Forum* (Indiana University Bibliographic and Special Series), 9, no. 15: 65–81.

—. 1994a. Review of Ralph Maud, *The Porcupine Hunter and Other Stories: The Original Tsimshian Texts of Henry Tate*. *American Anthropologist* 96: 10–11.

—. 1994b. 'Seven hundred million to one: making a difference in Alaska Native language and literature.' Keynote address to the Alaska Native Education Council, 8th Annual Statewide Conference, Anchorage, October 10–11, 1994.

Dorson, Richard. 1972. *Folklore and Folklife, An Introduction*. Chicago: University of Chicago Press.

Dundes, Alan. 1964. 'Texture, Text, and Context.' *Southern Folklore Quarterly* 28, no. 4: 251–65.

Eastman, Carol, and Elizabeth Edwards. 1991. *Gyaehlingaay/Traditions, Tales, and Images of the Kaigani Haida: Traditional stories told by Lillian Pettviel and other Haida elders.* Seattle: University of Washington Press.

Enrico, John. 1995. *Skidegate Haida Myths and Histories.* Collected by John R. Swanton; edited and translated by John Enrico. Skidegate, British Columbia: Queen Charlotte Islands Museum Press.

Foster, Michael K. 1974. *From the Earth to Beyond the Sky: An Ethnographic Approach to Four Longhouse Iroquois Speech Events.* Canadian Ethnology Service paper no. 20; National Museum of Man Mercury Series. Ottawa: National Museums of Canada.

Goldstein, Kenneth. 1964. *A Guide for Field Workers in Folklore.* Hatboro, Pennsylvania: Folklore Associates.

Hymes, Dell. 1981. *In Vain I Tried to Tell You: Essays in Native American Ethnopoetics.* Philadelphia: University of Pennsylvania Press.

–. 1987. 'Anthologies and Narrators.' In *Recovering the Word: Essays on Native American Literature,* edited by Brian Swann and Arnold Krupat, 41–84. Berkeley: University of California Press.

–. 1989. 'Tlingit Poetics.' (A review essay of Dauenhauer and Dauenhauer 1987) *Journal of Folklore Research* 26, no. 3: 236–48.

Jackson, Bruce. 1987. *Fieldwork.* Urbana and Chicago: University of Illinois Press.

Johnston, Basil. 1991. 'One Generation from Extinction.' In *Native Writers and Canadian Writing,* edited by W.H. New, 10–15. Vancouver: University of British Columbia Press.

Jones, Eliza. 1979. *Chief Henry Yugh Noholnigee/The Stories Chief Henry Told.* Fairbanks: Alaska Native Language Center, University of Alaska.

Kwachka, Patricia. 1992. 'Discourse Structures, Cultural Stability, and Language Shift.' *International Journal of the Sociology of Language* 93: 67–73.

Krupat, Arnold. 1989. *The Voice in the Margin: Native American Literature and the Canon.* Berkeley: University of California Press.

Lord, Albert B. 1965. *The Singer of Tales.* New York: Atheneum.

–. 1991. *Epic Singers and Oral Tradition.* Ithaca: Cornell University Press.

–. 1995. *The Singer Resumes the Tale.* Edited by Mary Louise Lord. Ithaca: Cornell University Press.

Mason, Phyllis. 1987. 'Read aloud Tlingit tales. A review of *Haa Shuká/Our Ancestors: Tlingit Oral Narratives,* edited by Nora Marks Dauenhauer and Richard Dauenhauer.' *The Midden* 19, no. 4.

Mattina, Anthony. 1987. 'North American Indian Mythography: Editing

Texts for the Printed Page.' In *Recovering the Word: Essays on Native American Literature*, edited by Brian Swann and Arnold Krupat, 129–48. Berkeley: University of California Press.

Maud, Ralph. 1989. 'The Henry Tate-Franz Boas Collaboration on Tsimshian Mythology.' *American Ethnologist* 16: 158–62.

–. 1993. *The Porcupine Hunter and Other Stories: The Original Tsimshian Texts of Henry Tate*. Newly transcribed from the original manuscripts and annotated by Ralph Maud. Vancouver: Talon Books.

Nida, Eugene A. 1964. *Toward a Science of Translating*. Leiden: E.J. Brill.

Ong, Walter J. 1975. 'The Writer's Audience is Always a Fiction.' PMLA 90, no. 1: 9–21.

–. 1982. *Orality and Literacy: The Technologizing of the Word*. New York: Methuen.

Ramsey, Jarold. 1983. *Reading the Fire. Essays in the Traditional Indian Literature of the Far West*. Lincoln: University of Nebraska Press.

Rothenberg, Jerome, and Diane Rothenberg. 1983. *Symposium of the Whole: A Range of Discourse Toward an Ethnopoetics*. Berkeley: University of California Press.

Sarris, Greg. 1993. *Keeping Slug Woman Alive: A Holistic Approach to American Indian Texts*. Berkeley: University of California Press.

Saville-Troike, Muriel. 1989. *The Ethnography of Communication: An Introduction*. 2nd edition. Oxford: Basil Blackwell.

Scollon, Ron, and Suzanne Wong Scollon. 1979. *Linguistic Convergence: An Ethnography of Speaking at Fort Chipewyan, Alberta*. New York: Academic Press.

–. 1981. *Narrative, Literacy, and Face in Interethnic Communication*. Norwood, New Jersey: Ablex.

–. 1984. 'Cooking It Up and Boiling It Down: Abstracts in Athabaskan Children's Story Retellings.' In *Coherence in Spoken and Written Discourse*, edited by Deborah Tannen, 173–97. Norwood, New Jersey: Ablex.

–. 1995. *Intercultural Communication: A Discourse Approach*. Oxford: Basil Blackwell.

Scribner, Sylvia and Michael Cole. 1978. 'Literacy Without School: Testing for Intellectual Effects.' Vai Literacy Project Working Paper No. 2. Rockefeller University, Laboratory of Comparative Human Cognition.

Sherzer, Joel, and Anthony C. Woodbury. 1987. *Native American Discourse: Poetics and Rhetoric*. Cambridge: Cambridge University Press.

Swann, Brian. 1983. *Smoothing the Ground: Essays on Native American Oral Literature*. Berkeley: University of California Press.

–. 1987. 'A Note on Translation, and Remarks on Collaboration.' In Swann and Krupat 1987, 247–54.

–. 1992. *On the Translation of Native American Literatures*. Washington: Smithsonian Institution Press.

–. 1994. *Coming to Light: Contemporary Translations of the Native Literatures of North America*. New York: Random House.

Swann, Brian, and Arnold Krupat. 1987. *Recovering the Word: Essays on Native American Literature*. Berkeley: University of California Press.

Tannen, Deborah. 1982. *Spoken and Written Language: Exploring Orality and Literacy*. Norwood, New Jersey: Ablex.

–. 1988. *The Argument Culture: Moving from Debate to Dialogue*. New York: Random House.

Tedlock, Dennis. 1983. *The Spoken Word and the Work of Interpretation*. Philadelphia: University of Pennsylvania Press.

Toelken, Barre. 1976. The 'Pretty Languages' of Yellowman: Genre, Mode, and Texture in Navaho Coyote Narratives. In *Folklore Genres*, edited by Dan Ben-Amos, 145–70. Austin: University of Texas Press. First published in *Genre* 2, no. 3 (1969): 211–35.

–. 1979. *The Dynamics of Folklore*. Boston: Houghton Mifflin Company.

–. 1987. 'Life and Death in the Navajo Coyote Tales.' In Swann and Krupat 1987, 388–401.

–. 1994. 'Coyote, Skunk, and the Prairie Dogs.' In *Coming to Light: Contemporary Translations of the Native Literatures of North America*, edited by Brian Swann, 590–600. New York: Random House.

Voegelin, C.F. 1954. 'Multiple Stage Translation.' *IJAL* 20, no. 4: 271–80.

Wallis, Velma. 1993. *Two Old Women: An Alaska Legend of Betrayal, Courage and Survival*. New York: Harper Perennial.

Watahomigie, Lucille, and Akira Y. Yamamoto. 1992. 'Local reactions to perceived language decline.' *Language* 68, no. 1: 100–17.

2 How do we learn language? What do we learn?

There are, of course, many ways a case may be argued or a thesis presented. The matter of establishing the bond between language and literature for the purpose of improving language instruction is no different. Language and literature may well be considered separate and independent, as if they were unrelated. But to treat these topics as if they had no bearing one upon the other is representative neither of the kinship between them nor of the manner of their growth and development. It is precisely because language has been separated from literature in Native language programs for teachers and students that language studies have by and large failed.

Were language to be considered not as an element unrelated to literature but as an integral constituent of it, the philosophic basis of language instruction would undergo change. And were such practical matters as the manner and progression of learning and the knowledge besides speech that is acquired in the course of learning a language taken into account, current methods and systems would be set aside and others more in keeping with the natural mode and order of learning language would be instituted.

The questions to be asked are, how do we learn language, and what do we learn from language? Think of how it was when you were a child; think of how it is with children. Think of how you learned your language, and think of what you learned. Think of how children learn speech.

Children do not have trained teachers; they do not have formal lessons; they do not learn in classrooms; they do not refer to texts; they do not labour over homework. They know nothing of grammar or linguistics, of phonics or sound systems. They have none of the advantages that second-language students have, of studying in private carrels and wearing headphones and following a program. Yet, they learn.

How can this be? How can a child, or anyone, learn without some preparation, without a scheme? I think that children learn easily and readily because they listen and give wholeheartedly of themselves to sound. Even while they are yet fetal beings, without any means of knowing the world outside the womb, it is said, and I believe, that children can hear. If that is so, then hearing may well be regarded as prior to and even more essential than are the other senses in learning. And hearing remains the principal means by which children get to know the world and the other beings in it during the first few months of their lives. For infants there is little else but sound and touch: they can only listen.

And what is it that the infant hears? What does an infant listen to? Initially, I think that a babe hears nothing but a cacophony of sounds, and is unable to distinguish the rustle of leaves from the crackle of fire. At first, to a baby, the peal of thunder, the pound of breakers upon a shore, and the drum of partridge wings will be the same, differing only in volume. They will hear the sounds of varying pitch and harmony, tone and intensity. But it is mainly the human voice that an infant will listen to. The mother talks, the child listens. The parents talk, the child listens. Parents and their friends talk, the child listens. Other children talk, the child listens. Other than crying and eating on occasion, the child does little else but listen.

Then, by degrees, the child begins to distinguish between one sound and another, and begins to understand that sounds have meanings and that sounds with meanings are words. The child may indeed learn that 'this is a foot' and that 'this is a hand' and that a distant bark is that made by a 'dog,' but for the most part the mother and the parents go about their business of talking about the day's events or telling stories in the evenings without explaining the meaning of words or discussing stories. To do so would be pointless to the child, but the child listens.

Then one day, perhaps one and a half years after its birth and after upwards from six thousand hours of listening, the child utters his first word, in imitation of his mother. What word the child utters is not important, nor is how the word is pronounced any more than cute. What is important and causes joy for the parents is that the child has spoken. And the point at which a child attempts speech for the first time occurs when the child's hearing has become acute enough to allow the child to discern the difference between sounds and when the child begins to understand that sounds have meanings; not before.

From the first word the child proceeds quickly to others, loosening his tongue in the process.

Still the child listens. In the days and months that follow, the child adds to his vocabulary and to his understanding, quickly and surely. No longer is his hearing and speech simple, but it becomes complex; the child's mind begins to grasp and form ideas.

That is how you and I learned our language; that is how other children learn their languages. And even when we knew something of words and ideas, still we listened. That is how it was in our youth, that is how it is with other children. When children's vocabulary is large enough, they begin to listen to stories, and they begin to learn something of their heritage and culture. And as children and youth learn their tribe's traditions and customs and understandings, they also learn more about their own language.

For our people, what the children and youth of one generation learned of the past and of the knowledge of the tribe came through story. By custom and tradition our tribal storytellers told certain stories only in winter. These winter night gatherings were more than storytelling socials; they were meetings in which tradition, heritage, custom and culture were passed on to the youth.

The old storytellers, old men and old women, must have been endowed with insight and originality to create stories that were both whimsical and full of meaning at the same time. They created comic characters, Nana'b'oozoo and Pukawiss, and they invented comic situations for human beings as well as for the deities; they envisioned manitous and monsters, and they described heroes and cowards. All of the storytellers had a way with words, minting new terms in the course of their narration by combining roots, prefixes and suffixes in new and unusual ways.

Listeners loved to laugh as much as they loved to reflect. First laughter, then thought. It is precisely because our tribal stories are comical and evoke laughter that they have never been taken seriously outside the tribe. They have been regarded as juvenile, fit only for juvenile minds.

But behind and beneath the comic characters and the comic situations and the comic descriptions exists the real meaning of the story. When the storyteller told of the great flood and the re-creation of the world from a pawful of soil obtained by the muskrat from the bottom of the flood waters, the storyteller was illuminating in the most dramatic way possible how men and women may create their beings and their spheres from the pawful of talent or potential lying within the depths of their soul-spirits. The storyteller was telling the story not so much to amuse children as to describe what the tribe understood of human growth and development. Or the storyteller may have recounted the story of Nana'b'oozoo's hunting expedition with the wolves in order to learn to hunt first hand under the tutelage of one of the foremost hunters in the forest. To hear how Nana'b'oozoo trips over his own tail or how he too soon tires in the pursuit of his quarry, a moose, and must rest, and how he will not follow the advice and the example of his tutor because his tutor is only a wolf, may be regarded as juvenile, but the story exemplifies an aspect of human nature that seems to apply to humankind in general. In recounting the story the narrator did not explain that Nana'b'oozoo was like every other human being in following his own inclination rather than the advice or the example of another being. Or that Nana'b'oozoo was no different from any other human being deluded by long bushy tails and speed and grace. It may have taken years and many stories, but the child would begin to see in Nana'b'oozoo human nature; the child would see himself and he would begin to understand why Nana'b'oozoo suffered misadventures. No one told the child what the stories meant. The storyteller did not explain that Nana'b'oozoo is every man, every woman. The elders did not comment on human conduct. To the storyteller and the tribe the story told itself. It was for the child and each individual to seek that morsel of understanding and to draw his own inferences and start fashioning his being and his world. And in letting the listener interpret his stories in his own way and according to the scope of his intellect, the storyteller and the elders of the tribe trusted in the common sense of the child to draw interpretations that were both reasonable and sensible.

In the coming years the child would elicit more and more meanings from stories and ever more quickly see the point in the story. When that child sat before the storyteller to listen to stories, that child gave his spirit and his mind and himself to the story and the storyteller. Next to the children sat adults who listened to the same story, who listened in their own way, as one day the child would listen, but for the present the child was hearing something new and fresh. As they listened to stories and learned about battles and migrations, about the origin of day and night or the meaning of the call of owls, children were also learning more language. They may not have known it but they were learning about the vitality of words as words took on different shades of meanings in different contexts or lost some meaning in still another context. The children may not have known it, but words take on new dimensions only in conjunction and by union with other words. A word may indeed have its own meaning, gender, habitat, mood, voice, and sound, but it is only in relation with other words that it can acquire greater sense and impart sense to other words. This, then is what children and youth and all of us learn about language in the course of a story.

Words have range but they also have limits to their meaning; they can express only so much, and I suppose that this is so because men and women have limits to what they can know and how they can describe it. The word *w'daebawae* describes the tribe's fundamental notion as to the limits of perception and description. *W'daebawae*, in its literal sense, conveys the notion 'he/she casts his/her voice to the very limits of its range.' It refers to what one can know and what one can say. When a man or a woman is said to be speaking to the ends of knowledge and to the ends of language they are said to be speaking the truth. According to this term, and according to the tribe, the best that a speaker can do and the most that the listener can expect is not absolute truth but the highest degree of accuracy. Besides, one's senses may be easily beguiled and even deceived by bushy tails. It is better to say that 'it appears to be' or 'it is said' or 'the probability is high that' as the old people used to do with *eedoog*. On learning that an acquaintance whom I had not seen for some years was in Toronto, I asked my friend what our acquaintance was doing. '*W'anookeedoog*,' my friend replied, meaning that our acquaintance was in all probability working. By nature the man was a good worker, and it would be hard for him to survive in Toronto without some occupation. However, there was a possibility that our acquaintance was not working. One could no more be sure about remote matters than one could say for certain that a person staggering down the road was inebriated. To the old people truth, insofar as a person could know and express it, was sacred. A person who spoke what was within his knowledge was trusted and respected; one who spoke about things he or she knew nothing of was said to be speaking in circles, *w'geewinimoh*.

A word is elastic. It changes form, it changes moods, it changes tenses. It even changes its own structure by adding to itself and sometimes by subtracting from itself. That is the magic and mystery of words, and yet children will understand that word, whatever be its size, shape or colour, from its place in a sentence and in the story. Eventually the child will get to know *w'inaendum*, which means 'he or she thinks,' whether it is commingled with or is garbled by other sounds. From *w'mino-inaendum*, *w'kitchi-inaendum*, *w'geezhi-aendum*, *w'mauni-aendum, w'kishki-aendum, w'maunaud-aendum, w'banaud-aendum, w'geemood-aendum, w'geebaud-aendum, w'moozhig-aendum, w'nishinaud-aendum, w'naunaugataw-aendum, w'zaum-aendum, w'nigaud-aendum, w'chaunim-aendum,* to other forms of *'inaendum,'* the child will know the meaning of the word, even though he has not heard it before. In the same way the child will learn, as I learned, that *w'abi-izhanh* means 'he/she comes here,' although *abi-* means in this place and *w'izhauh* means 'he/she goes'; as he will say *w'mino-nawae-aun* to mean to appease, without knowing that the essential meaning of the term is to 'good cheek' someone. One of the advantage of our tribe's language is that a speaker need not memorize all the words or have heard them all. He may need to memorize no more than a few hundred prefixes, suffixes, verbs and nouns, and yet he will have a vocabulary numbering in the thousands.

But more important than language itself was what the tribe, through its elders, intended for its youth and how best the tribe could prepare youth for the life ahead. Youth learned from the stories what to expect from life, what was good for the tribe, what for the individual.

It is clear that there needs to be order and control and discipline and some means of enforcing these, even in a small community. And the only means that the old tribesmen had of instilling in youth and in its members a sense of what ought to be done and what ought not to be done was through story, not only for the sake of harmony within the community but for survival itself. The tribe had no means of forcing its members to do what ought to be done except to instill in each person an intent to do what was best for the tribe, for the family and for the self. And if a tribal member flouted tribal custom or code, he or she might suffer no more than ridicule and at worst retaliation at the hands of a fellow tribal member, or retribution at the hands of an evil manitou.

It was taken for granted that men and women generally meant well. Perhaps it is for this reason that our ancestors called themselves and gave to our tribe the name 'Anishinaubaek,' the good beings. But it is also in the nature of men and women that they cannot keep their minds on their intentions. They discourage easily, but there are a hundred other reasons why men and women do not always fulfill their intentions or live up to their dreams and visions, or quite measure up to tribal expectations.

To represent this aspect of human nature the tribe invented or dreamed into being Nanabush. Nana'b'oozoo is full of good intentions. Nana'b'oozoo is a manitou, but even manitous, as our ancestors believed, were bound by human needs and passions and by physical laws of the world. The instant that he heard of the abuse of his people by the Weendigo, Nana'b'oozoo left his home and village to avenge his tribal brothers and sisters. When he got to the Weendigo's camp, Nana'b'oozoo dared the enemy warriors to battle, but, on seeing the evil aspect of manitous and their number, ran in terror for his own life. With winter coming on, the tribe's stock of food would not carry the people through the winter, and Nana'b'oozoo counselled rationing and sharing the meagre supply. But secretly Nana'b'oozoo had no intention of sharing his food. Later, all Nana'b'oozoo found was a pile of dried fungi where he had stored his own meats. For the rest of the winter, until the first berries ripened in spring, Nana'b'oozoo was forced to eat dried berries that he found still clinging to trees. Another time Nana'b'oozoo was worried that his family would suffer during the coming winter. He therefore asked the heron how he managed to catch fish so easily. The heron told Nana'b'oozoo how to fish, but warned him not to take any more than he needed. Nana'b'oozoo fished, but he could not be content with one fish; he had to have more and more and more at that moment, not tomorrow. During the night all his fish turned into ice. Nana'b'oozoo concocted elaborate schemes to reduce the time and the labour expended in hunting ducks. He wanted the entire flock, not just one. What better way was there than to steal upon them underwater, bind their legs together and then tow them to shore? But the moment that the ducks felt the tow-line, they took flight and bore Nana'b'oozoo into the skies. Nana'b'oozoo weakened, lost his hold and tumbled into a lake.

Nana'b'oozoo was dreamed into being, into the world of myth, and into the world of reality. But Nana'b'oozoo is myth only insofar as he performed the fantastic and the unbelievable; otherwise he is real to the extent that he symbolizes mankind and womankind in all their aspirations and accomplishments and in all their foibles and misadventures.

Some time after men and women get to know something of human nature and the codes that regulate human conduct, they also come to know tribal institutions and ideas, and beliefs that bear upon tribal customs, government and society itself.

No more than a few examples need be adduced to show what some of these tribal institutions are. Take the matter of the notion of property. For the Anishinaubae tribe, ownership of land was conferred by Kitchi-Manitou upon the Nation, and for as long as the Nation endures so long will it possess title and right to the land and a claim to the yield of the land, air, and waters. Only the Nation owned the land, only the tribe had a permanence commensurable with the existence of the land; the Nation is part of the land and cannot be regarded as separate from it. A person has tenure only during the course of his life, and a trust to care for the land and reside upon it for the benefit of the tribe and future generations, who in their turn will come into tenure and trust.

If there was little government, and if chiefs and their councillors who superintended the affairs of their communities had as their authority only their experience, knowledge, ability and character, there was little need for more government. Even if there was more need for more government, as the Anishinaubaek and their neighbours, the Six Nations Peoples, implicitly recognized in their institution of the Council of Three Fires and in the League of Peace, they would have always preferred less. It is not likely that the Anishinaubaek or their Six Nations neighbours would have surrendered their personal freedom or readily submitted to authority. Such was their conviction of their intrinsic worth and equality that the Anishinaubae peoples seldom deferred to naked authority or yielded their independence or entrusted their well-being to another except on special occasions and only for brief periods. In Anishinaubae eyes no man and woman was better than his compatriots. To this day, the Anishinaubae peoples' conviction in equality of worth remains as firm as it has always been, and their resentment of any intrusion upon their independence through the exercise of authority has not abated.

Action and wisdom and accountability were the stuff of men and women, chiefs and councillors. Next to deeds, what the Anishinaubaeg most respected was speech. Perhaps the Kiowa author and Pulitzer Prize winner N. Scott Momaday best expressed his tribe's regard for language: 'words were medicine; they were magic and invisible. They came from nothing into sound and meaning. They were beyond price; they could neither be bought or sold ...' To the Anishinaubaek and other tribes, words were no less medicinal. They too were medicine and sacred, bad and good; they could either injure or heal, offend or comfort, mislead or enlighten. And insofar as words move or inform, they are the creations of the speaker, reflecting his or her moods, sentiments and skill with ideas. And just as the medicine man or woman can heal only as much as his limited powers allow, so a speaker can impart only what is within his knowledge and articulate only what is within his command of language.

At best and at most, all that a speaker could attain or be expected to attain was the highest degree of accuracy in describing what was within his knowledge and experience. The person abiding by the principles of addressing only those matters within his knowledge and describing as accurately as his vocabulary enabled him or her was said to have spoken as far as he or she could cast his or her knowledge by means of words. And just as a medicine person administered his or her medicine only for the purpose intended, so a speaker took care to speak only about matters within his knowledge and experience. Of such a person, people said *'w'daebawae'*: 'he or she speaks the truth.' A person abusing the truth and language was ridiculed with *'w'geewinimoh'*: 'he or she speaks in circles,' as a dog barks in circles in uncertainty.

Much work and study remains to be done in order to understand Anishinaubae ideas and institutions. Until that study is done, the Anishinaubae peoples and their teachers cannot fully understand the philosophy or the philosophic basis for their institutions, cannot fully transmit them to their children. In the mean time, the Anishinaubae people must rely on European texts and authorities for information and interpretation concerning their heritage, and continue to teach their heritage in terms of canoe construction, food preparation, clothing styles, and subsistence patterns as if Anishinaubae institutions either did not exist or, if they did exist, they had neither merit nor validity.

In the course of learning language, much more than speech is received. In the study of language much more than the ability to utter words or to express simple wants and sentiments is expected. The end of language is to glean some understanding of the transcendental, the abstract, the world, life, being, human nature, and laws both physical and human-inspired – as embodied in literature. Only in the context of literature does language make sense; and it is only in the ambit of literature that language studies, courses and exercises find relevance.

KIMBERLY M. BLAESER

3 Writing voices speaking: Native authors and an oral aesthetic

For centuries our stories were passed in oral tradition ... With written language came the task of learning how to hammer the voice onto the page with these little nails called 'alphabet.'

Diane Glancy, *Claiming Breath*

1 Ideals of orality

The relationship between the oral tradition and the written word, between story telling and story writing and reading, informs all contemporary encounters with Native Literatures. As Brian Swann notes, 'No matter how we try to finesse the problem, the question of translation remains paramount. All other topics are subsumed in it' (1992, xvii). Contemporary Native authors work to translate not only language, but form, culture, and perspective. And within their written words, many attempt to continue the life of the oral reality.

The significance of such attempts was underscored for me recently when I heard Harold Scheub discussing his book *The Tongue Is Fire: South African Storytellers and Apartheid*. In explaining the relationship between storytelling and the revolutionary anti-apartheid movement, Scheub noted that the stories as they might be written down or published are only part of the total intended message. For political reasons they are, in fact, encoded with additional meaning, and the task of interpretation, the task of unravelling their significance or revolutionary meaning, rests with the listener or the reader. The stories harbour an absence which is really a presence, inviting or alluding to a greater political message. In that sense, the stories are, as oral literature has always been, alive.

When Acoma writer and activist Simon Ortiz edited the early collection of contemporary Native American short fiction *Earth Power
Coming*, he noted the grounding of the thirty-nine stories in 'the oral
tradition and its various aspects' and he, like Scheub, also acknowledged the supra-literary intentions of the works (1983, viii). In his
introduction, Ortiz makes a brief but powerful statement about the oral
tradition and its function in Indian communities:

> There have always been the songs, the prayers, the stories. There have
> always been the voices. There have always been the people. There
> have always been those words which evoked meaning and the mean-
> ing's magical wonder. There has always been the spirit which
> inspired the desire for life to go on. And it has been through the
> words of the songs, the prayers, the stories that people have found a
> way to continue, for life to go on. (1983, vii)

Ortiz then claims a continuation of that communal function in the written stories of the collection noting that the commitment by the Native
writers is not only 'a commitment to literature and writing,' but to
'something more serious than that.' Their goal, he believes, is 'to make
sure that the voice keeps singing forth so that the earth power will not
cease, and that the people remain fully aware of their social, economic,
political, cultural, and spiritual responsibilities to all things' (1983,
vii–viii). Survival or continuance, Ortiz claims, supersede mere entertainment as *raison d'être* in these works of fiction and in the literary
traditions from which they arise.

Likewise, Scheub spoke about the importance of the larger oral tradition to the survival of South African communities. Perhaps the construction of a tenured identity through storytelling creates a sense of
selfhood and community loyalty powerful enough to fuel survival.
Storytelling, he claims, 'weaves people into the very fabric of their
societies.' Through speaking, hearing, and retelling, we affirm our
relationship with our nations, our tribal communities, our family
networks. We begin to understand our position in the long history of
our people. Indeed, we become the stories we tell, don't we? We
become the people and places of our past because our identity is
created, our perspective formed, of their telling.

This communal identification comes about most fully when the oral
involves an active exchange, when it incites response or a sense of
response-ability in the listener.[1] Kiowa author N. Scott Momaday offers
a fine description of storytelling in his novel *House Made of Dawn*.

Through the Priest of the Sun's remembrances of his grandmother, Momaday comments on active listening as an important element of oral tradition. Storytelling, he explains, is more than speech; according to the old woman in the novel, it is both to 'utter' and to 'hear,' to 'listen' and to 'delight' (1966, 88). Ortiz, too, notes the importance of understanding and responsiveness in the oral: 'A story is not only told but it is also listened to; it becomes whole in its expression and perception' (1984, 57). And as participants in story, we must, Ortiz says, 'listen for more than just the sounds, listen for more than just the words and phrases'; we must 'try to perceive the context, meaning, purpose' (1977b, 9). The particular kind of engagement Ortiz and Momaday describe requires that we add something to the exchange, something not directly named in the language. That exchange, that involvement in story, what Anishinaabe author Gerald Vizenor calls dialogue and discourse, what Susan Brill calls 'conversive imagination,' what Mikhail Bakhtin calls 'utterances' – that giving, receiving, and giving back (or 'returning the gift' of story) – creates the reality or life of the story.

What a particular return involves varies with the circumstances of life and telling. The response might range from perception or simply acknowledging understanding, to engagement in a conversation or involvement in the telling of the story, to a more active taking up of the story in retelling, interpretation of the unspoken, or physically reacting through political resistance. Vizenor claims that these forms of interactive or reactive storytelling are 'not consumable.' Whether the listener's role is dictated by political circumstances which require the kind of encoding Scheub describes, or by an aesthetic history of participatory telling, or by any combination of these, the space left for response necessarily alters expectations of form and methods of presentation.

The ideals of participatory story, however, become more difficult to attain when cultures move from speech to writing. Can the dynamics of the oral exchange be duplicated or approximated in the written? Is this the aspiration of Native writers? Should it be? What differences exist between the attempts to re-express traditionally oral songs or stories in written form, and the attempts to write 'creative' works grounded in the tribal oral traditions or reflective of an oral aesthetic?

Although the cultural, linguistic and literary circumstances in which contemporary Native writers are reared vary, the descent from orality of Native literatures has resulted in a dedication to an oral aesthetic in the rhetoric, and sometimes in the written works, of many Native authors. Attempts to record the oral are always limited, but translators

of Native literatures and many contemporary tribal authors as well
work to retain the oral presence. They attempt to write in a way that
encourages re-speaking: the imagined rediscovery of inflection, gesture,
rhythm and so on. In this attempt, how words are written becomes
vitally important. As scholar Arnold Krupat has noted (1987), talking
on the page involves a delicate balance between fixing and unfixing
words and meanings, and it involves a cooperative venture between
writer and reader of nearly the same magnitude as the one that existed
between speaker and hearer.

Simon Ortiz encapsulates the attempt of many First Nations authors
today in a statement from his story 'What Indians Do.' The story is far-
ranging, discussing in turn the writing of a play, the alienated distance
in much of modern life, and the unique understanding inherent in certain Acoma phrases. When Ortiz describes 'what Indians do' at a pow-
wow, he might also be describing what Indians try to do in their
creative work:

> It's like a story being told when it's not only being told. The
> storyteller doesn't just tell the characters, what they did or said, what
> happens in the story and so on. No, he participates in the story with
> those who are listening. The listeners in the same way are taking part
> in the story. The story includes them in. You see, it's more like an
> event, the story telling. The story is not just a story then – it's occur-
> ring, coming into being. (1969, 104)

The events of oral tradition, the occurrences, the comings into being,
the community of story, these are the elements of tribal telling that
many Native authors attempt to incorporate into their written works.
Their goal, ultimately, is to destroy the closure of their own texts by
making them perform, turning them into a dialogue, releasing them
into the place of imagination.

Most scholars agree that the oral can never be fully expressed in the
written, and that experience cannot be duplicated in text. Context,
Native language, and Native culture ultimately cannot be translated.
While conceding these points, Native authors still believe in the importance of the attempt and in the possibilities for bringing the text to life.

2 Political and social contexts

Tribal authors pursue their art within a complicated set of circumstances or conditions. Native stories and identity, a 'commodity' for

years, have provided a wealth of 'material' for non-Native representation. Larzer Ziff claims that Native Americans were present in early American literature only through 'the white man's representation' and that what he calls 'the process of literary annihilation would be checked only when Indian writers began representing their own culture' (1991, 155). The impetus behind the works of many Native authors is exactly that of checking the process of literary annihilation and freeing Native American identity from the grasp of literary colonialism. To accomplish this liberation, American Indian authors often struggle against established literary and linguistic structures, practices, and images, and work to create new ones.

The tensions apparent in the American Indian authors' involvement with literary and academic pursuits arise from several cultural and historical intersections common to many tribes, and common as well, as Scheub's *The Tongue Is Fire* illustrates so clearly, to many other postcolonial cultures. 'The Indian author,' Choctaw writer and scholar Louis Owens claims in *Other Destinies*, 'is writing within the consciousness of the contextual background of a nonliterate culture' wherein 'every word written in English represents a collaboration of sorts as well as a reorientation (conscious or unconscious) from the paradigmatic world of oral tradition to the syntagmatic reality of written language' (1992, 6). These tensions between oral and written, and between English and Native languages, still have currency even though many Native American writers grew up with English and with the written mode, for a deep and affecting cultural investment in orality and Native languages remains. Indeed, the work of Indian writers contains many tangible manifestations of a commitment to as well as a descent from orality and Native speech patterns. But for anyone who professes the power of the oral and pursues the vocation of a writer, the inherent contradiction remains. 'The printed word,' Gerald Vizenor writes, 'has no natural evolution in tribal literatures' (1994b, 142). So, as Robert Silberman has said, 'There is something paradoxical about the attempt to keep alive mythical, oral values through literary ... means' (1985, 14).

The philosophical and practical dilemmas of writing are complicated yet further when the problems of translation – cultural and literary – are brought to bear. Kenneth Lincoln asks:

> How can the translator carry Native American oral traditions –
> hundreds of indigenous literatures permeated with religion, mythology, ritual, morality and heuristics, national history, social entertain-

ment, economic skills and magic formulas, healing rites, codes of
warfare and hunting and planting and food-gathering, visions and
dreams, love incantations, death chants, lullabies, and prayers – into
printed words in books for modern audiences? (1983, 25)

In fact, good intentions notwithstanding, translation itself, particularly
as it has been practiced in conjunction with Native American literatures, has come to represent a process of domination. It has in the past,
in principle, always tended to be the privileging of one language and
culture over another, and offered validation for the indigenous literature only as an object of study by the dominant culture, or, as Arnold
Krupat has noted, as an object of comparison, with the dominant
culture's models functioning as the master template (1992). Affected in
translation is everything from relatively isolated decisions about the
choice of place or personal names, to more broadly significant issues
involving the connotations of words or the symbolic value of colours
or creatures, to the extremely crucial selection and arrangement of
material and the shaping of the narrative frame of story. The effects of
these and other culturally determined aesthetic decisions cannot be
overemphasized.

In commenting on the issues of translation, Gerald Vizenor states
plainly that he does not believe Native traditions and literatures can
be translated. However, he believes they can be 'reimagined' and
'reexpressed' and claims, 'That's my interest' (Bowers and Silet 1981,
49). This process of re-expression, and the process of Native writing in
general, in most instances has meant writing in English, and often in
the literary and aesthetic forms of the dominant culture. As such, it
requires certain adjustments, and the use of select tactics to overcome
the inherent constraints. But with competence in the dominant language and familiarity with the expectations of the publishing industry,
contemporary First Nations writers have begun to involve themselves
in writing the voices of Native peoples, allowing them to be heard
with limited interpretation or translation. Native writers have learned
to use the literary forum to their own ends. They have, in Owens's
words, learned to 'appropriate ... tear free from its restricting authority,
another language – English – and ... make that language accessible to
an Indian discourse' (1992, 13). The self-conscious appropriation of
English for tribal use is wonderfully dramatized by Pawnee author
Anna Lee Walters in *Talking Indian* when she has one elderly character
tell a story and then reflect: 'Now I sit here, sixty years later, telling
you the exact same thing my old folks told me as a teenager. The only

thing that's different is I'm talking in a foreign language, one forced on us, but nevertheless, I'm still talking Indian. It's ironical' (1992, 41).

Gerald Vizenor, too, has reflected on the 'transformations' of the Native voice. The following passage comments on the historical realities involved in the determination of language, reveals Vizenor's own ambivalence about his relationship to writing in English, and alludes to a revolutionary vision that allows him to mitigate that ambivalence.

> The English language has been the linear tongue of colonial discoveries, racial cruelties, invented names, simulated tribal cultures, and the unheard literature of dominance in tribal communities; at the same time, this mother tongue of paracolonialism has been a language of liberation for many tribal people. English, a language of paradoxes, learned under duress by tribal people at mission and federal schools, was one of the languages that carried the vision and shadows of the Ghost Dance, the religion of renewal, from tribe to tribe on the vast plains at the end of the nineteenth century.
>
> ... English, that coercive language of federal boarding schools, has carried some of the best stories of endurance, the shadows of tribal survivance, and now that same language of dominance bears the creative literature of distinguished crossblood authors in cities ... The shadows and language of tribal poets and novelists could be the new ghost dance literature, the shadow literature of liberation that enlivens tribal survivance. (1994b, 162–3)

Vizenor envisions a powerful tribal literature capable of restoring the future to the 'vanishing race' of American history and literature. This 'new ghost dance literature' appropriates the written tradition and then re-creates that tradition on its own terms.

3 Writing voices speaking

The task facing Native writers, trespassing as it does on the grounds of so many political and cultural issues, becomes more difficult still. As a part of the process of halting 'literary annihilation' or as a part of what Vizenor calls the 'literary ghost dance,' many Native American writers have assumed a subversive stance with regard to issues of literacy and literary aesthetics. In their work, they often find themselves negotiating against the authority of the very written tradition in which they are engaged: challenging the rules of writing, challenging the truth of historical accounts, challenging the privileging of text. Their

own work often rewrites, writes over, writes through, writes differently, writes itself against the Western literary tradition. Native writers
often tell a different story, tell it from a different perspective, from a
different worldview. They challenge the reigning literary conventions
and the enshrined styles of writing both in principle and in practice.
Emma LaRocque, for example, comments on the connections between
enforced literacy and the First People's literary aesthetic and practice:

> Native Writers have a dialectical relationship to the English (or
> French) language. Not only do we have to learn English, we must
> then deal with its ideology ... We may ... disagree with what is aes-
> thetically pleasing. We may prefer Basil Johnston or Louise Erdrich
> over Stephen Leacock. We may bring our oratorical backgrounds to
> our writing and not see it as a weakness. What is at work is the
> power struggle between the oral and the written, between the Native
> in us and the English. And even though we may know the English
> language well, we may sometimes pay little attention to its logic –
> perhaps we will always feel a little bit rebellious about it all. (1990,
> xx–xxi)

LaRocque's comment suggests the kind of self-conscious subversion
that becomes its own art form. Native authors may challenge the 'logic'
of English in its basic structures. They also challenge and subvert the
acceptable literary forms.

Examples of this self-conscious subversion include the determined
use of 'Red English' or the playful engagement in what Keith Basso
has called 'code-switching' (1979, 8). Tom King's short story 'One
Good Story, That One' offers a fine example of the use of Indian
English, re-creating a certain recognizable way of speaking. The sound
of that voice supersedes every 'proper' rule of grammar or editorial
guideline for narrative presentation. The story opens:

> Alright.
> You know, I hear this story up north. Maybe Yellowknife, that one,
> somewhere. I hear it maybe a long time. Old story this one. One
> hundred years, maybe more. Maybe not so long either, this story.
> So.
> You know, they come to my place. Summer place, pretty good
> place, that one. Those ones, they come with Napiao, my friend. Cool.
> On the river. (1993, 3)

While this story represents 'Indian English,' others of King's stories make fun of the way non-Native people talk. The code-switching Basso describes among the Western Apache also includes the playful imitation of the voice and manner of the 'whiteman.' Of course, inherent in this kind of mimicry, he explains, is 'social commentary' (1979, 9). Rich with verbal play, Anishinaabe writer Gordon Henry's novel *The Light People* (1994) contains several examples of satiric code-switching. In a courtroom scene, for example, he imitates the rhetoric and manner of a museum curator while that curator speaks in defense of displaying a ceremonially dressed Ojibway leg. The presentation manages to subtly undercut the practice and the character of the curator, to challenge the philosophical underpinnings of the 'museumization' of culture, and to belittle the very language used: what Vizenor calls the 'manifest manners' of dominance. The subversions practiced by King and Henry base themselves upon knowledge of differing language models.

Native writing, however, does not always or even necessarily begin in conscious opposition to perceived imposed structures. We may instead view it as beginning with a dedication to a known pattern of rhetoric or story. Many authors, for example, begin first with a commitment to the intentions of the oral event, even in written text. For Gerald Vizenor, writing becomes a search for 'word cinemas.' He 'finds his place on the written page' not by abandoning the oral, but by his attempts to bring the oral tradition into his written works: 'What I go after that's like the oral tradition is I leave it open, I don't resolve it. Now that leaves open the possibility for discourse ... And that's liberating and healing' (Blaeser 1987). Other Native writers have undertaken similar attempts to imbue texts with orality. Simon Ortiz identifies his goals in *A Good Journey*: 'I wanted to show that the [oral] narrative style and technique could be expressed as written narrative and that it would have the same participatory force and validity as words spoken and listened to' (1977a, 9). N. Scott Momaday, too, has spoken of an attempt to 'bring those traditions [the spoken and the written] closer together' and says he believes they 'can be informed by the same principle' (Evers 1976, 21).

Can Native authors bring the principle of the oral tradition to the written? Perhaps a better question is, how do they try to bring talk off the page, or write voices speaking? If writing implies closure, perhaps Native authors work toward what Walter Ong calls 'opened closure' (1977, 312). Perhaps they seek what Elaine Jahner calls a 'specific kind of mythic "'breakthrough into performance'" (2). The nature of the attempts, of course, varies with the authors. Native authors may offer their story through multiple voices to create a cacophony of reality; range freely through the conventional boundaries of time and space to depict the interconnections of myth and present experience, of spirit and flesh; resist the arbitrary 'ending' of story to embody the continuance of life and telling; or bend their stories back on themselves, shape their tellings around circular visual images, the weavings, webs, or 'sacred concentricities' of their cultural and aesthetic experiences.[2] They may try to bring to their telling relatedness, we-vision, and earth voices. Leslie Silko's intermingling traditional myth with contemporary story in *Ceremony* creates a link with Laguna oral stories and tradition. Vizenor's frequent emphasis on the spoken – sound, conversation, telling – through verbal testimony, talk radio, fictional interview scenes, monologue, dialogue, letters, first-person narratives, lectures, political speeches, etc., re-creates the oral, the human voice, at every opportunity. Gordon Henry's creation of a collage of forms in *The Light People*, from drama to haiku to song to essay to ceremonial description, requires active participation of his readers in the making of story just as traditional oral narratives are often participatory.

Each of these aesthetic movements might be traced through the written works of multiple Native authors. The participatory quality, for example, characterizes much contemporary Native literature. Cherokee writer and scholar Betty Bell begins her novel *Faces in the Moon* with these words:

> I was raised on the voices of women. Indian women. The kitchen table was first a place of remembering, a place where women came and drew their lives from each other.
> ... They spent their lives telling stories ... The stories lived, never finishing in circumstance or death. Or even in the storyteller herself. (1994, 4)

Later in the novel, she writes:

> I listened, their stories settling forever in my blood, and I knew the stories were told and told not for carrying but for keeping.
> They heard, and they taught me to hear, the truth in things not said. They listened, and they taught me to listen in the space between words. (56–7)

In many ways, Bell attempts in *Faces in the Moon* to write not just words but voices, to make the text take on an oral quality. In addition to depicting voice dramatically, Bell also hearkens stylistically toward an oral aesthetic and thus for the audience engagement inherent in that medium. Her text encourages the reader to 'hear the truth not said' and to 'listen in the space between words.' For example, Bell's protagonist Lucie silences her mother's words when she literally burns her mother's attempt at autobiography. But this action hardly depicts the full and complicated loyalties, betrayals and contests that exist between the two women. We are not given the words Gracie Evers wrote, but Lucie symbolically takes up her mother's story. This understanding of the relationship, however, can only be garnered from both the written and the unwritten of the text. The 'whole truth' can only be arrived at by the effort of the reader and it is a truth meant to be passed on and lived, not consumed.

One critical study that offers a theoretical discussion of the methods specific to traditional Indian literatures is Jarold Ramsey's *Reading the Fire* (1983). Ramsey, too, comments on the minimalism of transcribed oral texts and how this minimalism necessitates active reader participation: 'One universal characteristic of the printed texts of the traditional Indian literatures is their tacit, economical texture ... typically, more is suggested in the withholding of narrative and descriptive details than in the outright rendering of them' (186–7). To explain one of the reasons for this minimalism, Ramsey uses the example of an encounter by the ethnographer Ruth Underhill with a Papago woman who, before providing Underhill with a version of a tribal song, explained, 'The song is very short because we understand so much.' Tribal telling assumes an acquaintance with and understanding of the tribal world view in which, as Ramsey says, 'so much [is] tacitly understood' (186).

But Ramsey and other scholars of Native literature claim that this minimalistic writing stems from more than the sense of 'cultural homogeneity.' The method is, in Ramsey's words, 'a deeply ingrained habit of the native imagination, with enormous implication for what modern Indian writers do with the stories they tell' (187). Native storytelling often self-consciously and purposefully proceeds by suggestion and implication because it thus becomes a dialogue or pluralistic creation. 'One is compelled,' Ramsey writes, 'to participate in the story, eking it out of what the characters say and what they do' (187).

Like Ramsey, scholar Lester Standiford draws a parallel between the 'dense holophrastic nature' of tribal language, the 'compactness of the literature,' and the 'embedding technique' and 'cryptic nature' that characterize contemporary Native American literature. He claims that this 'nondirective approach ... allows a reader the feeling and the meaning of the experience in his or her own turn' (1982, 185–6, 188). Kenneth Lincoln, too, discusses the tribal method of telling, saying that 'In general, a storyteller does not interpret or gloss the tale too much. Listeners imagine their participatory places in the story' (1983, 49).

Other literary scholars and tribal persons have also noted the minimalistic methods of traditional literatures. Lame Deer, in *Lame Deer: Seeker of Visions*, speaks of symbols and imagery in tribal life and notes, 'We need no more than a hint to give us the meaning' (1972, 97). Swampy Cree tribesman William Smith reveals much about both method and purpose in tribal storytelling with his comment: 'Maybe it won't be easy to hear, inside the story, but it's there. Too easy to find you might think it too easy to do' (qtd. in Lincoln 1983, 40). Here the medium enforces the message. We learn our role in story and are meant to carry that role into daily life. We have a response-ability and a responsibility to the telling. We can and we must make the story together.

4 Literary self determination

The rhetoric of an oral aesthetic is well established as are the characteristics many Native authors identify as distinguishing their work, linking their writing to the tradition and dynamics of spoken or performed tribal literatures. But are these works distinctly 'Native'? Are they, or how are they, distinctively 'oral'? Do their patterns have anything in common with Western aesthetic forms? With canonical non-Native writers? These questions are best asked about individual works and authors, and the answers, of course, would vary greatly. But perhaps these are not the questions that should be asked at all. Why must Native literature be described comparatively? Can it be validated as a genre only if it distinguishes itself from all previous and contemporary types of writing? Isn't such a demand merely re-creating in the literary arena the same cultural 'purity' litmus test once used to determine the 'real' Indians? We might do better to simply observe what various Native writers attempt in their work, to follow the shapes and alignments of each text, to hear the stories and learn their lessons.

But since the questions have been raised and will be raised repeatedly, I answer this: When students first read Native literature, they tell me it is refreshing or confusing or inspiring, but most of all they tell me it is different. In addition to content, the differences they point to have to do with style of presentation and demands made on the reader. Perhaps the multiple narrators of Momaday are like those in William Faulkner, the fluid time of Silko like that in Kurt Vonnegut Jr., the push for social action in Vizenor like the 'alienation effect' of Bertolt Brecht. Perhaps, too, the Ojibway dream songs are like imagist poetics; as Carl Sandburg sarcastically wrote, 'Suspicion arises that the Red Man and his children committed direct plagiarism on the modern imagist and vorticists' (255). Sandburg's comment, of course, playfully realigns the question of influence. But even that is not the point. We can concede influence and impurity and still have a recognizable tendency, a genre, or a school of Native writing.

There is a movement in Native written literature connected to its roots in orality. Attention to this connection has resulted in a certain style of writing. Tribally based aesthetic patterns may appear inadvertently in the work of some writers, quite self-consciously in the work of others. Regardless, Native authors show similarities in the way they attempt to encourage a response-able way of reading – an imaginative, interactive, participatory creation of story. More than that, I believe that Native literatures have supra-literary intentions. They want to come off the page and affect life. Leslie Silko's novel *Ceremony* (1977) enacts healing. Louis Owens's novel *Wolfsong* (1991) awakens our environmental conscience. Gerald Vizenor's *Harold of Orange* (1994a) requires we re-examine our neat stereotypes. Native stories have goals beyond entertainment just as their predecessors in the oral literatures did. They work to make us into communities, form our identity, ensure our survival. Native authors, like authors of many postcolonial cultures, write revolution; their 'tongue is fire.'

In Bell's *Faces in the Moon*, the character Lucie has an encounter with a white librarian. She has come to read the Dawes rolls, searching for her Grandmother's name. But his deprecating manner challenges her identity. Bell's character responds with fire:

> 'I ain't asking you to tell me who I *think* I am. I am the great-granddaughter of Robert Henry Evers, I am the granddaughter of Hellen Evers Jeeters, I am the daughter of Gracie Evers, the niece of Rozella Evers, and the grandniece of Lizzie Sixkiller Evers.'
> '... Let me put it to you this way. I am a follower of stories, a negotiator of histories, a wild dog of many lives. I am Quanah Parker swooping down from the hills into your bedroom in the middle of the night. And I am centuries of Indian women who lost their husbands,

their children, their minds so you could sit there and grin your shit-eating grin.'

'... I am your worst nightmare: I am an Indian with a pen.' (1994, 192)

Bell, like many Native authors, reclaims lost voices and in deft literary moves writes those voices 'talking on the page.' In their texts, Native authors have begun the revolution Vizenor calls a 'literary ghost dance.'

NOTES

1 I employ this term to represent a kind of world view, a sense of being responsible by being engaged in life processes, of having both the capability and the obligation to live this way. See my 'Pagans Rewriting the Bible' (1994).
2 Gordon Henry coined the phrase 'sacred concentricity' to describe the complex dynamics of circularity present in many Native stories. Whether the actual inspiration of that cyclical vision is a web, a medicine wheel, or another culturally significant image, Henry recognizes in Native life and work a sacred centre from which emanate ripples of power and connection. This centre (or these centres) are dynamic and thus invoke responses such as return, forgiveness, healing, vision. The mobile centre of consciousness might be a person, a place or an event; it might reflect the motion of the landscape, of seasons, or of families and communities.

WORKS CITED

Basso, Keith. 1979. *Portraits of 'The Whiteman': Linguistic Play and Cultural Symbols Among the Western Apache.* Cambridge: Cambridge University Press.

Bell, Betty Louise. 1994. *Faces in the Moon.* Norman: University of Oklahoma Press.

Blaeser, Kimberly M. 1987. Personal Interview with Gerald Vizenor. Berkeley, California, 27–9 May.

–. 1994. 'Pagans Rewriting the Bible: Heterodoxy and the Representation of Spirituality in Native American Literature.' *Ariel* 25, no. 1: 12–31.

Bowers, Neal, and Charles L.P. Silet. 1981. 'An Interview with Gerald Vizenor.' *Melus* 8, no. 1: 41–9.

Evers, Larry J. 1976. 'A Conversation with N. Scott Momaday.' *Sun Tracks* 2, no. 2: 18–21.

Glancy, Diane. 1992. *Claiming Breath*. Lincoln: University of Nebraska Press.

Henry, Gordon. 1994. *The Light People*. Norman: University of Oklahoma Press.

Jahner, Elaine. 'Heading 'Em Off at the Impasse: Native American Authors Meet the Poststructuralists.' Unpublished essay.

King, Thomas. 1993. *One Good Story, That One*. Toronto: HarperCollins.

Krupat, Arnold. 1987. 'Post-Structuralism and Oral Tradition.' In *Recovering the Word: Essays on Native American Literature*, edited by Brian Swann and Arnold Krupat, 113–28. Berkeley: University of California Press.

–. 1992. 'On the Translation of Native American Song and Story: A Theorized History.' In *On the Translation of Native American Literatures*, edited by Brian Swann, 3–32. Washington: Smithsonian Institution Press.

Lame Deer, John (Fire), and Richard Erdoes. 1972. *Lame Deer: Seeker of Visions*. New York: Simon and Schuster.

LaRocque, Emma. 1990. 'Preface: Here Are Our Voices – Who Will Hear?' In *Writing the Circle: Native Women of Western Canada*, edited by Jeanne Perreault and Sylvia Vance, xx–xxi. Edmonton, Alberta: NeWest.

Lincoln, Kenneth. 1983. *Native American Renaissance*. Berkeley: University of California Press.

Momaday, N. Scott. 1966. *House Made of Dawn*. New York: Signet/New American Library.

Ong, Walter J. 1977. *The Interfaces of the Word: Studies in the Evolution of Consciousness and Culture*. Ithaca: Cornell University Press.

Ortiz, Simon. 1969. 'What Indians Do.' In *Fightin': New and Collected Stories*. Chicago: Thunder's Mouth Press.

–. 1977a. *A Good Journey*. Tucson: Sun Tracks/University of Arizona Press.

–. 1977b. *Song, Poetry, and Language: Expression and Perception*. Tsaile: Navajo Community College Press.

–, ed. 1983. *Earth Power Coming: Short Fiction in Native American Literature*. Tsaile: Navajo Community College Press.

–. 1984. 'Always the Stories: A Brief History and Thoughts on My Writing.' In *Coyote Was Here: Essays on Contemporary Native American Literary and Political Mobilization*, edited by Bo Scholer, 57–69. Aarhus, Denmark: SEKLOS/University of Aarhus.

Owens, Louis. 1991. *Wolfsong*. Albuquerque: West End.

–. 1992. *Other Destinies: Understanding the American Indian Novel*. Norman: University of Oklahoma Press.

Ramsey, Jarold. 1983. *Reading the Fire: Essays in the Traditional Indian Literatures of the Far West*. Lincoln: University of Nebraska Press.

Scheub, Harold. 1996. *The Tongue Is Fire: South African Storytellers and Apartheid*. Madison: University of Wisconsin Press.

Silberman, Robert. 1985. 'Gerald Vizenor and *Harold of Orange*: From Word Cinemas to Real Cinema.' *American Indian Quarterly* 9, no. 1: 5–21.

Silko, Leslie. 1977. *Ceremony*. New York: Viking.

Standiford, Lester. 1982. 'Worlds Made of Dawn: Characteristic Image and Incident in Native American Imaginative Literature.' In *Three American Literatures: Essays in Chicano, Native American, and Asian-American Literature for Teachers of American Literature*, edited by Houston A. Baker, Jr., 168–96. New York: MLA.

Swann, Brian, ed. 1992. *On the Translation of Native American Literatures*. Washington: Smithsonian Institution Press.

Vizenor, Gerald. 1994a. *Harold of Orange*. Screenplay. In *Shadow Distance: A Gerald Vizenor Reader*, 297–333. Hanover: Wesleyan University Press/University Press of New England.

–. 1994b. 'The Ruins of Representation: Shadow Survivance and the Literature of Dominance.' In *An Other Tongue: Nation and Ethnicity in the Linguistic Borderlands*, edited by Alfred Arteaga, 139–67. Durham: Duke University Press.

Walters, Anna Lee. 1992. *Talking Indian: Reflections on Suvival and Writing*. Ithaca: Firebrand Books.

Ziff, Larzer. 1991. *Writing in the New Nation*. New Haven: Yale University Press.

J. EDWARD CHAMBERLIN

4 Doing things with words: Putting performance on the page

I am going to start right off by offending most of you.

'On the aforementioned occasion, the said Mr. Bruce did use the word cunt; and four times, the word fuck.' This was Lenny Bruce – dirty Lenny, as he liked to be called – speaking about himself on stage. Well, sort of speaking – for in fact he was reading from the transcripts of his latest trial, using the very same words he had been arrested, tried and convicted for speaking on stage some months earlier ... which were then dutifully written down in the official court transcript. And as he spoke again these written words, he set in motion another arrest, and another trial. How can it be *illegal* to read aloud a *legal* document? he asked (see Pechter 1989, Bruce 1963). How indeed? Where is the distinction between a word spoken, and the same word written? Where indeed? What *is* there about the power of the spoken word, and of performance? Wherein lies its exceptional power to offend? And what about the much touted power of the written word, and the page? Are the 'consequences' of a text, its practical effects and its theoretical implications, different depending on whether it is spoken or written?

Awkward questions. I regret to say that I have no easy answers. Just more questions. But they are ones that need to be on our minds as we go about the business of putting performance on the page. Let's stay for a moment on stage, and in court.

In one of the most celebrated cases in recent Native North American litigation, the Gitksan and Wet'suwet'en went to court in 1987 to demonstrate jurisdiction over their ancestral territory in what is now northwestern British Columbia, in the case known as *Delgamuukw v. the Queen*. Despite its focus on economic and political issues, the case was as much about language and literature as it was about law and the land, for the claims of the Gitksan and Wet'suwet'en were delineated by the songs and stories of their oral traditions, rather than by written documents. That turned out to be a problem.

Courts have a test that they apply in such cases called the 'organized society' test, requiring those who assert collective rights to demonstrate that they have a collective history. It's not as silly as it may seem, for almost all communities claiming a right to be heard accompany that claim with a demonstration of their social and political lineage, and their cultural heritage. Where Aboriginal people are concerned, courts seem to want proof that they have not only a continuous history but a *civilized* history as well. Unfortunately, one of the insignia of civilized status, at least for courts of European descent, is literature. Specifically, written literature. 'The plaintiff's ancestors had no written language, no horses or wheeled vehicles,' wrote the then Chief Justice of the British Columbia Supreme Court Allan McEachern, dismissing the case of the Gitksan and Wet'suwet'en in 1991. They must have 'roamed from place to place like beasts of the field,' he concluded, in one of the most brutish statements in current jurisprudence, one that resonates even since the Supreme Court of Canada's reversal of McEachern's judgment in December 1997. The immensely detailed, intricately patterned stories and songs in which the Gitksan and Wet'suwet'en recounted their ten thousand year history during a year of testimony did not convince McEachern of anything except their deprived and intermittently depraved condition.[1]

His is a sadly familiar response, and one that should trouble all of us; but along with righteous indignation, I want to display some sympathy with the dilemma in which the judge found himself, because it has a lot to do with the dilemma of editing Aboriginal oral texts. For a start, we might want to reflect on why anyone would want to edit and print Aboriginal oral texts. The reasons are various, and they are not particularly colonial or postcolonial. First of all, there's the desire to preserve stories and songs, and to codify agreements and occasions in a written or material form. This is an Aboriginal as well as non-Aboriginal urge, as non-alphabetic forms of writing such as beads and strings and carvings and paintings and petroglyphs and pictographs and chests and blankets attest. It doesn't always work in one direction, of course. Many societies, again both Aboriginal and non-Aboriginal, commemorate certain occasions by turning *written* into *oral* texts. This is especially true of sacred occasions, but it has secular counterparts as well. Words of power, whether spoken or written, have one thing in common. We remember them; and often we remember spoken words better than written ones. The words of prayers, curses, proverbs, names of peoples and places.

My favourite example of the dilemma an editor can get into when trying to turn one kind of text into another comes from a quite different tradition. We are familiar with books being turned into films. This was one of the occasions when a film was turned into a book – a great book, as it turned out, but one which almost gave its author – we might as well call him an editor – a nervous breakdown. The book is *The Harder They Come*, by Michael Thelwell; and it was inspired by a film with that title written by Perry Henzell and Trevor Rhone and directed and produced by Henzell, which told the story of a legendary Jamaican reggae songwriter, ganja trader, and gunman named Rhygin, played by Jimmy Cliff. Cliff also, of course, wrote and sang the title song. The book's use of local language – specifically Rasta or 'dread' talk – had considerable influence on the development of fiction both in the West Indies and as far away as Australia, where the Aboriginal writer Colin Johnston – Mudrooroo – acknowledged Thelwell's inspiration.

In an article about the 'translation' of the film to the novel form, Thelwell recounts his experiences and his apprehensions. He quotes a particularly revealing conversation that took place when he was about half way through the writing.

It was by way of a phone call from Jamaica: quite literally the voice of the audience, and calling about the work too!

'Breddah Michael, we hear say you writing a book, is true?' The caller was Brother Sam, poet-historian and theologian-in-residence with the Mystic Revelations of Ras Tafari, the very influential cultural ensemble centred around the master drummer and Rasta patriarch Count Ossie, who had recently died. Naturally I was surprised and very pleased – vindicated really – by this unexpected expression of interest from this militant of grass-roots culture. I started to babble on about how very touched I was that he had called all this way and to explain the project, only to be cut off. (The call was, after all, much too expensive for pleasantries.)

'Dass all right Breddah Mike. Soun good, de book, is bout us, right? Den dat mean the Count mus in dere, seen?' The phrasing was a little ambiguous, a question but not a question. It was too early. I wasn't quite sure I understood. So he explained.

'I an I the brederin hear say you doing dis mighty work, seen? Well den, we the brederin checking to mek sure that Count Ossie will get his due and rightful place derein. So long as is about us, the Count supposed to be in dere. True?'

'Wait, is dat you calling me for?' The tone of hurt indignation was not just tactical on my part. 'My brother, you really believe say I could write a book about yard, and leave out the Count?'

'Well, not to say you would leave 'im out, but ...'

'Well, you can tell the brederin that the Count will certainly be in there. Seen, Iyah?'

Then, realizing that I might be making too hasty and sweeping a commitment, I felt compelled to launch into a discussion of the constraints of literary form. I explained at some length, and into a silence that somehow seemed to deepen as I spoke, that were I indeed doing a social or cultural study Count Ossie would inevitably have to be a major figure. Which was quite true. But this was a *novel*. And while I would wish the Count to be in it, and would certainly put him in if it proved possible, it would have to fit the context, and I couldn't categorically guarantee that the opportunity would present itself, or that if it did the Count would be as prominent as the brederin would wish. So much depended on the dictates of form, considerations of narrative structure, historical chronology, and the like.

'Surely you understand, my brother,' I implored into the by now unnerving silence, fully aware of how fatuous and arty-farty I sounded as my words echoed back to my own ears. But in Sam there was neither mercy nor absolution.

'Understan?' he mimicked contemptuously. 'Understan what? Stan under you mean. Iman must *stan under* say de man *want* to give praises and thanks to the Count, but it depen pon *form*? Pon *narrative struckchah*? Pon *fictional integrity*? Tell me something, mi Lion?'

'Yes?' I asked timidly.

'Tell me dis – is who writing who? *Is you writing de book, or de book writing you?*'

And he did not wait for an answer, a kindness probably not intentional. For a long time after that, I was haunted by a vision of Sam dramatically recounting our conversation to the assembled brederin and concluding with apocalyptic solemnity, 'Our brederin gaan. Him laas. For is truly written, 'Many a foolish and heedless Ithiopian shall go down wid Babylon.' (Thelwell 1991, 150–1)

With this example we have a good illustration not only of the challenges of cross-cultural translation – and a good part of Thelwell's dilemma had to do with whether and how to translate the more impenetrable elements of dread talk (the film is often shown dubbed for non-Jamaican audiences) – but also of the second reason editors do what they do: to make a text either *more* available, to widen the audience; or *less* available, to narrow the audience. Plato, that old marginal man living on the edges of Europe and Asia and Africa, disdained writing because it encouraged what he called promiscuous readers: anyone could read what you wrote, while only the chosen could listen to what you said. Others, of course, have seen opportunities in the written word where he saw problems – opportunities for making texts available to different generations, for example. Others again have seen writing as a way of limiting access to an essentially mandarin community, rather than expanding it in a democratic way.

Third among reasons to transform performances into writing is the one Judge McEachern identified: to demonstrate that you are an organized society. It's obviously contentious to claim this as a reason for putting performance on the page, because it is so bound up in the contemporary politics of colonial privilege in which writing is the mark of civilized status. But in fact it has for a long, long time been just as prominent a reason for putting the page into performance. The display of oral traditions of story and song, and of written traditions of narrative and lyric – as well as of a wide range of other discursive forms (such as woven and beaded belts and blankets; carved and painted trays, poles, doors, verandah posts, canes and sticks, masks, hats, and chests; and so forth) – turns out to be one of the time-honoured ways in which societies (as well as groups within societies) affirm their identity, establish their history, demonstrate the intellectual and emotional integrity of their critical and creative practices, and exhibit the character of their intellectual and emotional lives. The organized societies test, as it were, is not limited to the courts. It is routinely invoked by many people, much of the time, to get recognition and to maintain authority. This is true not only in such obviously political forms of expression as creeds and constitutions, national anthems and national histories, but in other forms of expression, as groups – women and blacks, to take a couple of obvious instances – demonstrate their collective presence by showing that they have a literary tradition. Part of this is of course documentary. But partly too it's to pass a kind of organized societies test. Serious societies – and groups within society that want to be taken seriously – have a literature of their own, the argument goes; and a history too, each with its own distinctive forms and sometimes even its own distinctive languages. These languages are not necessarily either spoken or written.

They may be differently performative – dancing and drumming, perhaps – and even if written, they need not be in alphabetic form – quilts come to mind, and Peruvian *quipu*, Iroquoian condolence canes, and Chilkat robes. But they will almost certainly constitute what we might for convenience call a literature, in that they will embody a set of stories and songs in and through which the defining meanings and values and experiences of the group are represented, and (no small consideration) the group's identity advertised.

The urge to tell stories and sing songs, like language itself, is a defining quality of human societies – a boundary marker between the human and the nonhuman, and between different societies. These stories and songs may display differing attitudes towards everything from personal identity to social property. But they will almost certainly be markers of who we are, and where we belong. The Canadian geographer Peter Usher tells about a meeting between an Aboriginal community in the northwest and a group of government foresters. It was about jurisdiction over the woodlands. The foresters claimed the land for the government. The Tsimshian were astonished by the claim – they could not understand what these relative newcomers were talking about. Finally one put what was bothering them in the form of a question. 'If this is your land,' he asked, 'where are your stories?'

This question was only superficially about property. There was something more. The member of the band who asked that question was also asking those government foresters, 'how do you think and feel?' Or perhaps, as you might ask of people whose membership in the human race has come into question because of their odd behaviour, '*do* you think and feel?' For just as different languages determine different thoughts and feelings and forms of behaviour, so do the stories and songs to which they give form. If these languages, and therefore the stories and songs, are radically different one from the other, the groups will identify a corresponding difference in the way each thinks and feels ... and maybe *whether* they do either. Except for the power relationships involved – and ultimately it's impossible to ignore these, I admit – the stereotyping of Aboriginal peoples as savages by the early settlers according to the way they spoke, the stories they told, the songs they sang, and the way they behaved, is fundamentally not all that different from the stereotyping of settlers by Aboriginal peoples now – as linear, chop-logic thinkers with feelings confined to limited categories, the acquisition of material goods, and no spiritual understanding whatsoever.

At the end of the day, I believe, these differences have much less to do with whether the languages are spoken or written than with the particular languages themselves, and with the different ways in which they negotiate between the authority of experience and the authority of the imagination. Cultures are not oral or written. Their most important forms of expression sometimes are.

It's time to go back to that courthouse in Smithers, where the stories and songs of the Gitksan and Wet'suwet'en were presenting some of these problems to the judge. Accustomed to direct testimony and written documents, McEachern initially applied the venerable hearsay rule to render inadmissible their traditional oral forms, the *ada'ox* and the *kungax*. Discounting the reliability of indirectly obtained evidence is not only a malicious modern practice, of course; nor is it the monopoly of those with power and privilege. In Europe, its use can be traced back to the middle ages, where it provided heretics with one of their main lines of defence. In its contemporary form, the exclusion of hearsay derives from a couple of concerns: that the court – or any community of listeners – cannot assess for itself the truthfulness of the original utterer, or story teller; and that the memory of what we have *heard said* is less reliable than the memory of what we have *seen done*. Both of these are obviously problematic, but they certainly are not by definition racist and reactionary. Rather, they are epistemological, having to do with how we know, and what it is that we know when we know.

After much contention, Judge McEachern relented on his application of the hearsay exclusion; but misunderstandings continued to plague the proceedings. It is sometimes said – Giambattista Vico said it first, and Northrop Frye repeated it (1982, 17) – that we should think of God (or the creator) as a verb, not a noun. It was as though the Gitksan and Wet'suwet'en spoke in verbs, and the court expected nouns. This provides a nice image for the challenge facing editors of Aboriginal oral texts. It's not that Aboriginal languages and traditions are verbal rather than nominal – quite the contrary, in many cases. But editing them is sometimes like changing all the verbs into nouns, and vice versa. Or to put it differently, it's like trying to eliminate the uncertainties and ungrammaticalities of one kind of language by replacing them with the fixities and correctnesses of another. If it weren't so vulnerable to a taxonomy of the primitive and the civilized, I'd say it's like trying to turn poetry into prose.

There was a moment in the case that exemplified the predicament. One of the Gitksan elders, Antgulilibix (Mary Johnson), was telling her *ada'ox* to the court. At a certain point, she said that she must now sing a song. The judge was flummoxed by a request that seemed to flaunt the decorums of his court. He tried to explain how uncomfortable he felt having someone sing in his court. He tried to make the plaintiffs understand that this was unlikely to get him any nearer the truth that he was seeking. He asked the lawyer for the Gitksan whether it might not be sufficient to have just the words written down, and avoid the performance. But finally, in the face of a dignified intransigence, he agreed to let Mary Johnson sing the song. Just as she was about to start he fired his final salvo. 'It's not going to do any good to sing it to me,' he said. 'I have a tin ear.'

His comments, both during Mary Johnson's oral testimony and in his written judgment, have been roundly castigated. But Judge McEachern was right. He did have a tin ear; and more importantly, he said so. That puts him a cut above most of us, who go through life – and who teach in the academy – assuming that we could make not only music but meaning out of Mary Johnson's song. This is a strange and, for the Mary Johnsons of the world, a sinister, assumption – an assumption that understanding complex oral traditions comes naturally to the sympathetic ear. It doesn't. Just as we learn how to read, so we learn how to listen; and these learnings do not come naturally. Nor are they the same across different traditions, listening to which may be as different as reading English and Chinese and Arabic. Few of us would suggest that reading is the same thing as seeing. And yet we routinely operate as though listening were the same as hearing. I don't mean in our everyday affairs, though it is undoubtedly true there; but in the ways in which we respond to the stories and songs of peoples for whom speech seems more important than writing, peoples whose traditions of imaginative and historical and philosophical expression are primarily oral rather than scribal, or at least verbally rather than visually performative ... though as soon as I say this you can recognize the problem, which is that verbal performance is always in some sense visual, if only by virtue of the presence of the performer. And all peoples *can*, in some sense of the word, read. No society would last long without a sophisticated ability to read the weather and the stars and the land and the water and the movement of fish and game, and to interpret the messages they provide from the natural or supernatural world – though these forms of expression often require a differently (though no less sternly) schooled skill in seeing and hearing.

Furthermore, oral traditions are certainly *not* all the same, and we cannot listen to them all in the same way. Nor should they all find the same sort of written form, obviously. Listening and watching – and sometimes touching and tasting and smelling that gooood grease, and doing so not just carefully but *properly* – is what Aristotle called the final cause of, in this case, editing Aboriginal oral texts in written form. It's what gives meaning to the exercise, its ultimate purpose.

The efficient cause, on the other hand, the actual mechanism which makes it happen, isn't just finding the right form into which to translate these experiences. Or rather, it is just that, but not in a narrow sense. It's finding what I call a *ceremony of belief* that accompanies the *chronicle of events*. This involves one very simple, but very difficult, task: getting the reader or listener to the point where they confront what the east coast writer and critic Robert Finley calls a moment of nonsense, a moment in which they are faced bluntly with the need to believe – or more exactly with the challenge 'believe it or not.' This has to happen right away, or *nothing* will happen. It is the key to editing – and indeed to reading and listening to – any text; but it is especially true editing an oral text, partly (and paradoxically) because of the very presumptions of transparency and truth-telling we sometimes associate with direct spoken testimony.

'Nonsense,' Judge McEachern says to Mary Johnson when she asks to sing her song. He was, in a serious sort of way, right so far. 'Unbelievable,' he says of her performance. Something went badly wrong. But 'unbelievable' is what we too may say of all kinds of performances if we're not in the proper state of readiness; which is to say, if we haven't taken ourselves through that moment of nonsense. There can be cultural resistances, of course; but in my experience they are much less formidable than the resistance presented by ubiquitous and perennial but not necessarily culture-bound patterns of thought and feeling, conventions of behaviour, and what I would call habitual rhythms and melodies of the imagination: listening for the flute when there's only drumming; or reading for a story when the text offers a song; or looking for a lesson where there's really a joke.

Poetry should help us with this, for it routinely demands that we suspend our expectations and our disbelief, or hold belief and disbelief in balance. A poet can say 'I saw Eternity the other night' (Henry Vaughan) or 'I like a look of agony' (Emily Dickinson) or 'So much depends upon a red wheelbarrow' (William Carlos Williams) and we nod our heads in agreement and delight. Another person might try this, on another occasion, and folks in white jackets would come to take him or her away. Editors need to have an answer as to why they shouldn't take the poets away, and why the judge should believe Mary

Johnson. Not too good an answer, for that would eliminate the possibility of what Coleridge used to call their dear gorgeous nonsense. But an answer that will get us to it, and through it. For that is where the real power lies, in the deeply irrational, unparaphrasable mystery of songs and stories.

There are tricks of the trade. As medievalists such as John Leyerle have pointed out, the intricate interlace designs with which ancient Celtic and Scandinavian societies decorated their oral and written texts reflected the character of their stories and songs, whose non-linearity in turn imaged the societies' sense of life, and land, and literature. So too with Yoruba tray carvings, Kwagewlth bead work, and so on. What sometimes appears to be on the physical margins often turns out to be at the spiritual and intellectual centre. The texts that have come down to us with these sorts of marginal decorations and sometimes musical notations provide a good example of how to instruct readers in the rhythms and melodies, the logic and the lines, of discursive traditions. They signal narrative, lyric and dramatic modes with what sometimes seems like ostentatious naiveté; but these *are* crucial categories, related to questions of who is speaking, and to whom, and about what. These also indicate, sometimes in physical ways, how audiences should respond: whether they should figuratively (and sometimes literally) kneel, sit, stand, fight; and whether they need to bring certain assumptions about personality or process into play. This cueing of the audience is the key. And it is an editor's responsibility to provide this key if people are not to find themselves in the situation of Judge McEachern, looking for a story when he was listening to a song.

Verbal and visual arrangements, including drumming and dancing as much as design and decoration, can be a like a tuning fork, giving everyone the right key for the story or song. Tuning up those tin ears. This is a central function, of course, of the regalia accompanying various kinds of performance, from Mary Johnson's *ada'ox* and the liturgical exhortations of a Christian preacher to the proscenium arch in a theatre and the layout of a book. Training of various sorts *can* help here – including training in illustrated manuscripts, illuminated books, and now CD-ROMs – as well as a fundamental understanding of the rigorous discipline of performance in different Aboriginal societies, including their often powerfully sensuous dynamics. Much contemporary criticism is so preoccupied with encoded meanings and deep structures and political themes that it forgets about these surface features, forgets even about the textures of the language itself, and the sounds and sights, the touches and tastes and smells that are part of its performance. As C.S. Lewis used to say, what is on the surface is not necessarily superficial at all. It may well be the deepest part of the text. Catching its character and quality in an edited text is profoundly important.

But it isn't easy. Part of the difficulty has to do with cultural and linguistic relativism. Put in its starkest form: different languages and different cultures 'experience' reality differently. How to carry this across is a continuing challenge. One of the possibilities that was proposed in the design of the Aboriginal History Project that I coordinated for the Royal Commission on Aboriginal Peoples was to bring different kinds of mappings into the foreground as part of the text itself, drawing attention to radically different classifications of land and water, for example, and of flora and fauna, the natural and the man-made, the spiritual and the material. Perhaps it might be useful to describe, inevitably rather briefly, that project and some of the lessons learned.

It began, in the usual way, as an injunction to rewrite history – to put it right in writing, to tell the true story, to affirm the position of Aboriginal peoples in the country. Since that position is *sui generis* – anomalous, like nothing else – so must their histories be. *Histories*, not history. That was the first hurdle. The key was to find a way of addressing three fundamental challenges: the diversity not just of Aboriginal cultures but of the form and function of their histories; the importance of representing this diversity in genuinely Aboriginal discourses, undistorted by the pressures of either colonial *or* anti-colonial polemic; and the debilitating effect of historical studies that homogenize Aboriginal experiences, exoticize Aboriginal traditions, and plagiarize Aboriginal voices.

When I say we, I include a loose array of Aboriginal and non-Aboriginal elders, tribal and academic historians, anthropologists, geographers, mapmakers, filmmakers, tribal leaders, lawyers and artists, many them deeply involved over a very long period in the development of strategies for nourishing Aboriginal oral traditions, and finding ways of putting their performance on the page. Discussions took place over nearly two years in large and small settings,[2] and were often extremely awkward – the awkwardness playing itself out, not surprisingly, across Aboriginal cultures (and gender and class and generation) as well as between Aboriginal and non-Aboriginal participants. At the end, we came up with a plan that would draw on the extensive work done already by the Gitksan and Wet'suwet'en, on the one hand, and the Labrador Inuit on the other, to provide (in book and accompanying map form) models for a series of volumes in an Aboriginal History series – the whole of which would be complemented by a major Aboriginal Atlas project, to reflect the importance of space/place as well as of time in the expression of Aboriginal histories. The Atlas would also develop new ways of representing the network of relationships to land and to the natural (and supernatural) world that is part of the historical consciousness of many Aboriginal peoples. It would take advantage of new technologies for this representation, and of the significant historical data already developed in Aboriginal communities by (among other things) the various mapping projects of the past twenty-five years. An inventory of place names would be a key part of this project, to give expression to the fact that the land upon which we live is, in a fundamentally historical sense, Aboriginal land; and that the languages of this land are Aboriginal languages.

Thus planning for the Aboriginal Atlas began with the importance of mapping Aboriginal names. And then it moved to a broader line of logic that went something like this. If people do not understand the nature of Aboriginal attachment to land – its complexity, its diversity, the ways in which it is not expressible according to the categories non-Aboriginal people (representing a long heritage of agricultural as distinct from hunter gatherer consciousness) usually use to classify and explain such things – then they cannot understand the experience of Aboriginal peoples, including their experiences of conflict. An Atlas, especially one that included a strong historical dimension, could provide a powerful, and a popular, way of conveying this.

The plan was that such an Atlas would incorporate Aboriginal classifications as a base, to give new perspectives on the land, its resources, and the changes that have taken place. It would show how different Aboriginal cultures perceive the same phenomena differently, and how much of the landscape is the product of Aboriginal ingenuity, from the rice fields of northern Ontario to the many spaces cleared (and now often assumed to have always been clear) for purposes of hunting, gathering, farming and fishing. And it would map the creation stories, as well as the great epic voyages and voyages of discovery, made by Aboriginal people.

The idea of beginning the Aboriginal History series with the Gitksan and Wet'suwet'en and Labrador Inuit volumes emerged out of the circumstances of the past twenty-five years, some of which led to the court case I have been describing. Since the early 1980s, Gitksan and

Wet'suwet'en elders and historians had been gathering, reading and analyzing their people's history. In particular, they had assembled many of the *ada'ox*, those records of crucial events and territorial exchanges from the earliest times, at least until first contact, charting the region's history from their own point of view. This rich body of cultural knowledge had already been used for public purposes, notably as evidence in the *Delgamuukw* case, which drew as well on a wide range of other historians' testimonies, and on their researches into Euro-Canadian archival sources. The Gitksan-Wet'suwet'en tribal council also oversaw, in the late 1980s, the preparation of a cultural atlas for their region. All these materials would provide the basis for this first volume in the Aboriginal History series. Those from the community who had been most directly involved in that work over the past decade, including tribal leaders Don Ryan and Neil Sterritt, indicated their support for this project; and a detailed plan (involving continuing consultation with elders and other custodians of Gitksan and Wet'suwet'en history) was prepared by Richard Overstall, Susan Marsden and Richard Daly.

The Labrador Inuit History presented a different kind of opportunity to bring together the historical research, the archival material and the community resources that had been developed in recent decades by and for the Labrador Inuit, and to bring to the foreground a history of a people that is unlike any other in the country. In 1975–6, the Labrador Inuit Association had conducted an extensive Land Use and Occupancy Project. This involved preparation of detailed historical and cultural maps, as well as extensive individual and family histories. This work was done in all the Inuit and settler communities of the northern Labrador coast. A striking feature of the work was scrupulous inclusion of settler families, all of whom, in this region, have close historical links with Inuit, in many cases going back 150 years. (Some settler families speak Inuktitut, as well as, or in preference to, English.) Also as part of the Labrador Inuit Land Use and Occupancy Project, the Moravian Periodical Accounts were culled for insights into Inuit experience in the 19th and early 20th centuries.

Some of the results of all this work were published by the Canadian government in 1977, in the report *Our Footprints are Everywhere: Inuit Land Use and Occupancy in Labrador*, edited by Carol Brice-Bennett. But this rich historical resource has never been made fully available. Moreover, the historical research in Labrador has continued to the present. As in the case of the Gitksan materials, there was a solid and accessible basis here for one of the first volumes in the Aboriginal

History series. Carol Brice-Bennett, drawing on her involvement in this work over the past two decades, agreed to prepare a detailed plan for discussion with the community and the Commissioners.

Immediate subsequent volumes were to include the Plains Cree and the Metis. A Plains Cree history, it was felt, would provide a different set of opportunities, and a different range of methodologies. There are well-developed community resources, including archival collections, to support this; the choice of the Plains Cree (rather than the Swampy Cree or the Woodlands Cree) reflected the resources immediately available not only in order to make the project more manageable but to provide in a timely fashion another model that might be useful for other Aboriginal peoples contemplating a project for the series. Stan Cuthand agreed to develop the idea, in consultation with elders in the communities, since he was meeting with a number of them at a gathering in Lac La Ronge during the summer of 1993; and Winona Stevenson and John Milloy were consulted about the project, which it was envisaged would in due course take shape with their advice.

A Metis history presented a set of daunting challenges; but most of the historians consulted felt that a project could be designed that would make a new and substantial contribution both to the historical understanding of the Metis and to a sense of the Aboriginal history of Canada. There are obvious problems of definition with the Metis, changing over time under the influence of changes in Canadian constitutional, legal and political practice, as well as in historical approach; there are stubborn and often acrimonious debates between historians; there are issues that open out into the broader history of the Americas. One idea (proposed by the prairie historian Gerald Friesen) was for a volume that would be along the lines of 'Voices of the Metis'; and of course there were other suggestions. Plans for further volumes – including histories of the Blackfoot and Iroquois confederacies, among other peoples – were being developed, each chosen for the way in which they would offer quite different models of historical expression, and different opportunities for the finding of written forms for the oral texts.

Thematic approaches for the initial volumes – relationships to the land, interrelationships between peoples, regional differences – had immense and immediate appeal. But in every case, problems quickly arose because of the complex and contentious character of these themes – a signal of their centrality, of course, but also a sign of the difficulty of accommodating them within texts that would provide a new kind of historical discourse. Furthermore, the tendency for such texts to be determined by very few people, inevitably representing only relatively few cultural experiences and historical traditions, was deemed to be overwhelming; and the possibilities for countering this tendency – having a wide range of voices and discourses in the texts, introducing contentious dialogues or debates into the narrative – presented problems, especially at the beginning of an historical project that was intended to generate a series of texts to continue well beyond the life of the Commission, and to constitute a significant legacy of historical, cultural, and political liberation for Aboriginal peoples.

And so each of the initial volumes was to be shaped *by* the oral traditions themselves, each with its defining Aboriginal discourse, its own particular forms of storytelling and singing, its own historical form and function. The authority and authenticity of each volume would derive from the particular historical discourse – the voices, the occasions, the confusions and contradictions – of the people whose history it embodies. There could be no single model: the oral traditions of the Iroquois are significantly different from those of the Blackfoot, which are different again from those of the Dene or the Gitksan or the Kwagewlth.

And the time frames would vary in accordance with each tradition. Most of the Gitksan and Wet'suwet'en history would be what is misnamed pre-history – that is, history that is not written down, history prior to European contact. In the detailed outline of the Gitksan/Tsimshian peoples' volume, Europeans appear in the eleventh of fourteen chapters – a bit early, but there you are. Furthermore, *recent* history in this volume would be presented *in the form* established by the Aboriginal traditions – in this case, the *ada'ox* – rather than in the form established by European historical practice. In this way, the imaginations of readers would be educated in Aboriginal conventions – educated in the forms as much as in the facts – by the particular text itself ... and thereby prepared for the next volumes in the series. This would be important, not just for non-Aboriginal but for non-Gitksan and Wet'suwet'en peoples, and indeed as well for some Gitksan and Wet'suwet'en for whom this volume would provide a way into their own history.

We got a long way towards this, but at the end of the day it didn't fly. The Commissioners, having put substantial funds towards the development of the project, would not put up the money to take it through the next phase. But it wasn't really about money. We had a generous and flexible publishing contract in hand from one of the country's major publishers for the whole open-ended series, including development funds and the offer of resources towards further fund-raising for the very expensive Atlas project; and a firm guarantee that each volume would be autonomous and Aboriginal centred – that is, Aboriginal conceived, designed and undertaken. And we had several other publishers bidding for it.

We had tried to accommodate the priorities rightly identified by the Commissioners: the debilitating and diverse legacies of colonialism; the deeply held but differently expressed relationships to the land; the variety of cultural and geographical experiences; the complex traditions of oral and written historical expression in Aboriginal and European languages, as well as in those which incorporate non-linguistic forms. The privileging of one account over another, the privileging of written over oral traditions, the privileging of metropolitan and academic historical criteria over the longstanding historical conventions of local Aboriginal communities – these are the pernicious legacies of settler history, which need to be revised and reversed. But simply reversing the roles in some generalized reaction against this may do little more than encourage a kind of essentializing and exoticizing and homogen-izing of Aboriginal voices. And revising the record, while it may replace one orthodoxy with another, also maintains the role of the metropolitan tradition as the certifier of standards. The fact that it can occasionally be persuaded to change its mind does not diminish – indeed in some respects can only enhance – its authority. After all, is there a more obvious, or a more intimidating, exercise of authority than the decision *not* to exercise it?

What was most problematic, we felt, was the habitual privileging of *events* over *words*. We wanted to turn that upside down. This is where the issues of historical theory and practice come into clearest focus, and into clearest conflict. History – the history we were being presented in performance – is primarily about *words*, not events. A revision of events, a recovery of Aboriginal particulars and priorities and perspectives with regard to events, would *not* in itself restore the authority of Aboriginal peoples over their history – which is to say, over their own forms of imaginative self-representation. Indeed, it might well perpetuate the current practice of ignoring divergent traditions of history among different Aboriginal groups, many of whom identify and interpret the 'same' events quite differently. A catalogue of events is not the burden of history. It is the burden of those who remember the events, neither more nor less. That can be a heavy burden, to be sure, especially when the events are distorted and discounted or discredited. But revising those events within a historical tradition that continues to distort and discount and discredit the words in which these events are told will provide only very temporary relief from that burden. And in any case, the remedy for the dispossession of Aboriginal historical discourses, and therefore of Aboriginal history, may ultimately lie less in recovering the realities of the past than in encouraging the imagination of those who will shape the stories in the present.

The development of a much greater (and much older) sense of common cause between historical and artistic expression seemed to us fundamental to the flourishing of Aboriginal history, and to recovering something of the traditional convergence of verbal and visual forms of representation. Because this would necessarily draw on a wide range of indigenous traditions of imaginative expression, many of which are being revitalized by a new generation of performers, it could stimulate the involvement of younger Aboriginal people in the process of shaping modes of self-representation, which may otherwise remain in hands of the older generation, exercising what the recent General History of Africa, in its deeply informed discussion of oral traditions and elders, called 'vieillesse oblige.'

Put bluntly, the Royal Commission didn't buy this. They wanted – and more power to them – to put things right. They wanted recommendations to that end. They wanted to be in control of the process. In fairness, I should say that several of the Commissioners argued passionately for it ... but to no avail. Some of it has taken on a life of its own anyway, and parts are moving ahead in their own way, at their own pace. What we have lost is a critical mass of undertakings, and the encouragement that mass could have given to each and every person involved.

In closing, I'd like to emphasize one distinction which in my experience can easily get lost in any discussion of expressive forms and cultural identity and how language does things as well as means things: that is, the ways in which what are sometimes called 'speech acts' function. By speech acts, I mean things like praying and preaching, cursing and praising, betting and promising, bearing witness and giving evidence, pronouncing sentence and professing truths, saying 'I do' or 'no' or 'I love you.' The distinction that gets lost is not exclusive to either oral or written traditions; but it manifests itself differently in each, and our critical practices lead us to recognize it differently. It is the distinction between the ways in which texts *express* or proclaim meanings and values, and the ways in which they *reveal* them. In case you think we don't use this distinction every day, consider the reasons why we insist that witnesses tell their stories in person. One reason, of course, is so that they can *express* their evidence in their own words; the other is so that they can *reveal* to us – by their demeanour, by the dialogue that ensues under cross-examination, and so forth – whether what they say is true. Written texts, also, both express and reveal their messages. Many of our most fruitful insights over the past decades have come from a renewed understanding of the ways in which the encoding and inscribing of texts reveal truths of which the author may be unaware, or may be trying to hide. New Criticism, the interpretative practice which flourished in the first half of this century and in which textual evidence was a fundamental tenet, may offer a useful corrective. It is often criticized for its failure to take context into account. But as many scholars familiar with oral traditions argue, New Criticism needs revisiting at least for its insistence on the *surface*, or texture, of a text – its recognition, to draw on Marshall McLuhan's phrase, that the medium is the message. As the anthropologist Renato Rosaldo insists, and Julie Cruikshank has wisely reminded us, we need to get back to that simple discipline of looking at (and listening to) texts, rather than always looking through or around or behind or underneath them. This is not easy. We are increasingly trained to look for transparency of story and of song. But it is the opaqueness of singing, and of story*telling*, that is at the heart of many oral traditions. Or to mix up the images, the ways in which they show, rather than tell.

Riddles provide a nice example of this balance between expression and revelation. They also offer an illustration of how we go into and through that nonsense moment I talked about, surrendering to the language, suspending one kind of belief for another; and how editors may be able to take us to that moment, right back to the roots of language and literature where we embrace the radical impossibility of metaphor and the radical illogic of representation. Let me give an example of a riddle that catches something of this, put by a bunch of young boys to Homer, the legendary poet and by reputation the wisest old man in ancient Greece. It was used by the American poet W.S. Merwin as the epigraph to one of his books, and recounted with rare insight by Robert Finley. It's kind of a hunter gatherer riddle, and it goes like this: 'What we've caught and killed we've left behind. What has escaped us we've brought with us. What have we been hunting?'

Homer couldn't solve the riddle, so the story goes; and he was deeply upset, not so much because of his inability – he was much too wise to be bothered by that – but because of the dilemma he now faced. Let's think about it a moment. Homer knows – this is the convention of riddling – that what the boys tell him is true. But he can't make sense of it. He knows all about hunting; he knows all about the world, in fact; and he knows what they say is nonsense. And yet he also knows it's *true*. The stakes are higher than they might seem. He has either to change his understanding of the world – an understanding that's served him pretty well up to now – or he has to solve the riddle. Fish or cut bait ... when there's nothing else in the world to eat but fish.

Eventually he solves it, with a little help from the boys. They've been hunting lice, it turns out, body lice on themselves. The lice that they caught and killed they left behind. What escaped them they brought with them. Language put Homer in the dilemma; and language – a word, in fact – got him out of it. But the dilemma was real. It involved a framework, in this case hunting, within which words were to be understood; and a challenge to Homer's understanding of what happens within that framework – what happens, that is to say, when you go hunting. In a way, it's an image of the real dilemma facing every editor, especially every editor transforming oral into written texts. At some point or other, we find ourselves in Homer's predicament, where we must find a word – or in our case, a form – that will resolve a deep contradiction. We need to hold on to what we know – that's something we must not ignore. But we also need to find a form, a framework, in which we can once again believe what we hear and see. We must find what the nineteenth century sage John Henry Newman used to call a Grammar of Assent. A way of saying yes.

Robert Finley's essay in which this riddle appears is nicely titled 'The Charm of Riddles,'[3] which reminds us that charm is there too ... charm, which derives from a root (carmen) meaning song. And just as Judge McEachern was wanting to keep himself free of the nonsense of Mary Johnson's riddle, so he was professionally suspicious of rhetoric, wanting to protect himself from its charms. No wonder he got anxious when Mary Johnson sang her song.

Something more than mere faith, more than a lively imagination, is required to understand Mary Johnson's song. It's what Northrop Frye used to call an educated imagination. I'm not sure most of us could have done much better than the supposedly learned judge. We might have behaved better, of course; but our good manners would only have masked our ignorance, and made us hesitant to ask some troubling questions – such as what is it, exactly, that would be lost if Mary

Johnson were to write down her song? What is the nature of our belief in words; and is the knowledge we derive from them the same whether they are spoken or written? The judge said that he believed Mary Johnson, but not her *ada'ox*. This is not as stupid a statement as it seems. The locus of belief has long been disputed, with consensus only that it hovers somewhere between singer and song, teller and tale. For editors of Aboriginal oral texts, it also hovers between speech and writing.

Put differently, the truths and beauties and goodnesses of a text – the elements to which we give assent – are not underwritten by its Aboriginal origins or the insistence of its author, but by its language and its style, its verbs and its nouns, its ceremonial requirements (the appropriate people speaking and singing in the proper places with their customary chests and blankets and headgear). These constitute the tradition itself, and it is the tradition that generates and guarantees the orderings of its stories and songs – their truth, their beauty, their goodness. It certifies or 'backs' them, the way gold or the government or the GNP back coin and paper currency, or the bank certifies a cheque – assuring us that credit is justified. And the word credit, after all, means simply he or she believes.

The question of what to believe, and whom, has obviously preoccupied both literary and legal theory for a very long time. In different forms, it preoccupies members of *any* community every time it tries to determine the truth. And so communities establish certain criteria for passing judgment, and develop a consensus (or conspiracy) of sympathetic understandings. Sympathy and judgment are the points of reference here, though they are obviously anything but fixed. Stories told in certain traditions are true because they are acts, creations, makings; in other traditions, because they are representations, imitations, mirrorings. The event to which a story or song refers may be either the original or the inspiration. And the proprieties of telling the tale may be radically different – for example, one passionate and possessed, the other straightforward and rational. The balance between spontaneity and style we ask of those bearing witness in church or in court, for example, illustrates the subtle relationship between convention and candour that gives witnesses credibility. A singer or a storyteller becomes believable when his or her language is accepted *both* as an expression of the tradition within which belief has become customary, and as (in some sense) the witness's own words (or the words of the witness in his or her ritual role), authentic and authoritative. (In a written tradition, the negotiation is between literary and local languages.) Asking which gives credibility to the other is like asking whether the individual gives meaning to the group, or vice versa. It depends. The editor's task is to make sure readers and listeners are aware of the difference, and are able to say 'that rings false' or 'that rings true' after a reasonably full engagement with the text, rather than constantly deferring to the editor's exhortations or to the politics of dispossession and dislocation.

NOTES

1   There is a fair body of material now available regarding this trial, beginning with the trial transcript itself. BC *Studies* devoted a special issue (Autumn, 1992) to the trial and judgment, with interesting articles by Julie Cruikshank, Dara Culhane and Robin Ridington, among others; and there is a book of excerpts, cartoons and commentary from the trial compiled by Monet and Skanu'u (1992). The most powerful single monograph is Pinder (1991). The text of the December 11, 1997 Supreme Court decision is available on the internet at: www. droit.umontreal.ca/doc/csc-scc/en/rec/html/delgamuu.en.html.

2   A major workshop was held at Nakoda Lodge in the Stoney Nation in Alberta in February, 1993. It included Michael Asch, Hugh Brody, Lorraine Brooke, Marlene Brant Castellano, Julie Cruikshank, Stanley Cuthand, Jean Morisset, Leslie Pinder, Tony Snowsill, Neil Sterritt, Winona Stevenson, Jacob Thomas, Peter Usher, and Ted Chamberlin. A Report, written by Ted Chamberlin and Hugh Brody, was submitted to the Commissioners in April. It provided an outline of three components – Aboriginal History, Aboriginal Atlas, and Aboriginal Historiography – which formed the basis for the development (at the request of the Royal Commission) of the detailed Aboriginal History series proposal over the following months. This project proposal was put to the Commissioners in October, 1993.

3   At time of writing, this essay had not been published. I refer to it with the kind permission of Robert Finley. The riddle appears in Merwin (1967).

WORKS CITED

Bruce, Lenny. 1963. *How to Talk Dirty and Influence People*. Chicago: Playboy Press.

Frye, Northrop. 1982. *The Great Code: The Bible and Literature*. Toronto: Academic Press.

Merwin, W.S. 1967. *The Lice*. New York.

Monet, Don, and Skanu'u (Ardythe Wilson). 1992. *Colonialism on Trial: Indigenous Land Rights and the Gitksan and Wet'suwet'en Sovereignty Case*. Gabriola Island: New Society.

Pechter, Edward. 1989. 'Of Ants and Grasshoppers: Two Ways (or More) to Link Texts and Power,' in *The Rhetoric of Interpretation and the Interpretation of Rhetoric*, edited by Paul Hernadi, 39–54. Durham: Duke University Press.

Pinder, Leslie. 1991. *The Carriers of No: After the Land Claims Trial*. Vancouver: Lazara.

Thelwell, Michael. 1991. '*The Harder They Come*: From Film to Novel. How questions of technique, form, language, craft, and the marketplace conceal issues of politics, audience, culture, and purpose.' *Grand Street* 37, 135–65.

VICTOR MASAYESVA JR.

5   It shall not end anywhere: Transforming oral traditions

Although it was delivered as an observation during song-making sessions, I took it to be an admonition as well when my Guardian said recently, 'This Hopi language will end, possibly for the recording of everything.' I thought perhaps he was referring to the belief prophecying the dissolution of the Hopi language and saying that our preoccupation with recording the language was hastening the process. But since it was not in the nature of our relationship for him to scold me I knew he meant me to 'be there, feel the song and Know' and not only to learn the words but to fully internalize the language in the old way. Fourteen years earlier, another storyteller had told me in referring to the videotaping of his stories, 'This will not end anywhere. You will continue to expand on it'; and so I have. These apparently contrasting statements illustrate the dilemma facing every Native American language preservation project with which I have been familiar: maintaining an oral tradition without interference from recorders and enabling instruction through mechanical proxies are not obviously compatible projects.

I have attempted to resolve this personal quandary by returning to principles of tribal sovereignty. It has become a question of sovereignty for me if I am to continue to live with the appearances, transformations and translations native to film, video, computer bits and the English language, from and through which I make my livelihood.

1 Sovereignty

In matters of politics, economics, and culture, it is a sovereign matter to insist on the right to one's own laws and processes of retribution. For example, the removal of Hopi religious images could be viewed as the kidnapping of a living being. Similarly, real estate transactions could be carried out with full regard for the way I value land, which is that land has no monetary price. Language is a sovereign matter as well. You cannot learn, speak, nor mean it for me.

However, sovereignty on reservations is quixotic. For some at Hotevilla, my birth village, sovereignty is an act of resisting electricity, running water and modern conveniences, but like other communities we have chosen to live within the boundaries of our reservations; we have not homesteaded on our Aboriginal lands or chosen a livelihood solely from the earth. Through loyalty to other tribes involved in gaming we have tacitly accepted gaming and the intercession of the state in our affairs. We allow federal courts to adjudicate crimes against humanity even when our own humanity is at stake. We allow the government to regulate our rivers, forests, air and the soil beneath our feet. Apparently, sovereignty is negotiable and plastic in this age.

We have also negotiated and commodified culture and language, contributing to a National Museum of the American Indian, and allowing Native American languages to be brokered and bid for by preservation initiatives. Our only excuse and reprieve from self-flagellation can come from the acceptance of our tribal members as colonized people: we do as the white people have done, writing, recording and presenting our own cultures outside of acknowledged traditional practices. As the world Turners so do we.

2 Indigenous expressions

Oral traditions are the expression of a tribe's sovereignty in matters of culture and beliefs, encapsulating the totality of its understanding of life and living. The expression of our understanding of life is in the conception of our language.

The prototype Hopi language for me derives from the chiefs' speech and song (*Mong lavayi* and *tawi*) which I hear articulated today in various cirumstances. My understanding derives solely from moments of ritual and ceremony when I hear those words and those songs as they are involved in the fulfillment of Life – language as creation in a procreative sense. When this sacred speech is created or sung in its proper place and time it must be entire, not interrupted or containing truncated feelings. It must surge forward as if it were the life-breath itself, as if keeping the physical body alive were dependent upon our words. It is creation itself, which cannot be interrupted any more than a cell can disrupt its own development process. This language in its essence is breathing, living, going forward, not arrested breath and death.

I think of the Hopi language at its most rudimentary level as expressed through agricultural manifestations, where everything that affects the ceremonial cycle – the earth, sun, clouds, moons, heat, moisture and the weather from the seasons past – is invoked. In that scenario everything is alive, developing, becoming, whether it is the buildup of the clouds and the beings that move in, with and through the turbulence, or the sentient seed. Nothing is static.

Language from agricultural traditions grasps the fecundity, the fertility and florescence, and becomes growth. In the desert, language becomes rain. When we speak this experience and breathe this creation we also become part of it and we move through this experience, Life, and become part of it like the bee – a pollinating being, planting, nurturing, harvesting – or like a rainfall. In speaking creation we become of it. The Hopi language is of the rains. Similarly, the language of a hunting people might have a hunting inspiration.

Now if language is living and we sever its agricultural wellspring, its source of inspiration and influence, we speak a dead language whose only purpose is that of communicating non-agricultural business and mostly engaging in transactions of oppression and indoctrination: do this, do that, where questions are not encouraged. In fact people are too intimidated to ask. Because most of us speak English in the workplace where we spend at least eight hours of each day, this dead language has saturated our mother's voice. We hear it in the morning on radio and television. We hear it on radio and television before we go to sleep. We hear it, speak it, and speak it, hear it, endlessly!

My generation understands English imperfectly but enough to tyrannize a household with a good 'god-damn!' and a 'shit!' or to poke fun at our accent and pronuncation: 'My kids don't respect me. They call me Daad' (pronounced 'dead' in Hopi English). My generation sings the Hopi morning songs of my parents' generation but not as publicly or robustly for fear of being thought drunk.

Mostly, severed from our agricultural roots, we are left with the shell of a language used primarily for the adornment of ceremony. In this way we have lost language, life, and creation. Today our phrasing, our meaning, is delivered truncated, rude, and with little grace and goodwill. Gone for my generation are daily and constant communication in Hopi and the ability to creatively make, use, and formalize new words and thus describe new concepts in Hopi.

Now when we record our language, we have begun the post-mortem, reserving and stacking the words which one now sees imprinted on the paleolithic bookshelves which accumulate sediment. We will resurrect knowledge from these shelves on occasional expeditions but we will not receive experience.

Now when we record language we relinquish meaning for cadences, rhythms and 'da da da da da,' catchy and meaningless. Not to say that 'da da da da da' when sung is not meaningful when it serves melody. It is said that pow-wow singing around the drum has become that way, soundful and wordless.

Some of us are involved in preservation, well meaning, but preservation. It is as if we had even lost the will to let things go, whether it be rituals, ceremonies, songs, or language. But what is left of our sovereignty if we allow non-community members to record, learn, speak and express our Selves? What has become of our communities if we encourage outsiders to determine our priorities and what is important to our communities? Is it not better that we do it ourselves?

3 It will not end anywhere

Language is a sovereignty concern of profound importance. You cannot learn, speak nor mean it for me. But you can understand it with me. In fact your involvement is essential to my indigenous expression. Needless to say sovereignty is possible only because of another sovereign. This then is how I have come to resolve the dilemma. In order to continue to be a part of my community and the larger community, every day is one of translation, negotiation, and choice. I cannot function in the community, in any community, as a self-contained ectoplasm.

Each new medium of conveyance, whether it be the English language, video, film, theatre, music and song, each and every one poses a tremendous challenge to the tribal person. Knowing what I know and what I want others to understand, how do I present my knowledge so that the expression will be known? The tribal translator must have quantitatively more knowledge than the Traditionalist and be more agile than the colonist to be understood in the world of engaged communities, both Hopi and non-Hopi. It is said of the clowns that they must be more acrobatic than the acrobats to work their magic. It is true of the tribal person's trans-performances as well in order that the inherited skill and ancestral knowledge will shine through the masks.

That it will not end anywhere is certain. Equally certain is that it will end, if we don't understand what we are working with. There are numerous examples of dead ends, superficial, lifeless, irresponsible, harmful and unaccountable derivations of tribal experience which are held up by investors and entrepreneurs as exemplary models of authentic tribal experience. These stand out and caution us against more recordings. But those that are successfully expanded have accountability as part of their understanding, for the sources of experience that inspired the original tribal community are acknowledged and invoked to inspire a larger community.

Today we have an older generation to whom the land is the bank, the shape of our currency, and yet we have foregone it for hourly wages. Now we are dependent upon and governed by the American currency, not reciprocal exchanges with the earth and natural forces, nor clan obligations and community obligations. We expect to be paid in dollars! With this passive acquiescence we are fulfilling the u.s. ideology of a melting pot and we as unique tribes are becoming an amorphous pan-Indian tribe adopting u.s. customs, including language, which is good for economics and politics but deathly for Culture.

Each unique tribal language is not a profane utility, basic human protocol, or the polite forms of etiquette and translation, but the language of intercession by which we are heard by the ancients. Language is living as only you individually or tribally can experience tribal living. Sovereignty in matters of culture and language: you individually and as a tribal member will not let it end ... anywhere ...

JULIE CRUIKSHANK

6 The social life of texts: Editing on the page and in performance

During the last two decades, I have spent considerable time thinking about issues at the centre of this conference. From the early 1970s until 1984, I lived in the Yukon Territory and had the good fortune to work with elders engaged in the project of recording their life stories. They and their families wanted to see accounts written in their own words describing memories and experiences spanning almost a century. Ongoing discussions about how these words should be recorded and transcribed on the page were central to the process we followed in trying to develop a shared ethnographic authority.

Then in the mid 1980s, I returned to university as a student after fifteen years absence, hoping to learn more about how varieties of knowledge passed on in oral narrative could enlarge scholarly understanding in anthropology, history and literature. There I encountered voices from all over the world – Africa, Australia, Europe, North and South America, New Zealand, Asia and the South Pacific – addressing questions similar to those we were asking in the Yukon about how oral tradition is becoming central to the project of translating 'culture' to larger audiences. Both these educational processes – in northern communities and in southern libraries – provide me with more questions than answers for our discussions this weekend.

This conference provides an opportunity to discuss a paradox that alternately troubled and exhilarated me during those years. On one hand, we all acknowledge that written, textual transcriptions of spoken language have the potential to freeze, or arrest speech. In the words of two of our participants, Nora and Richard Dauenhauer, 'The writing down of oral literature, no matter how well intentioned or how well carried out, petrifies it. It is like a molecule by molecule replacement of an organic plant by stone. A petrified log may look like wood, but it is actually stone' (1992, 16). On the other hand, during my years of living in and now regularly visiting the Yukon, I continue to marvel at the social life transcribed texts gain in the communities where they originate and continue to be told. I am especially intrigued by the ways Yukon elder storytellers point to writing as just one more way to tell their stories and to make them part of larger social processes. Written texts become points of reference to which narrators can allude when they want to make socially significant statements to family members, to other members of their community, or to the larger world about the potential of stories to make us reevaluate situations we think we understand.

Nora and Richard Dauenhauer argue that the study of oral tradition differs from other kinds of scholarly textual study because oral tradition is embodied; that is, it occurs in real time, it is performed, it always involves interaction between teller and listener, and in northwestern North America it is deeply embedded in clan and community. They suggest that as 'culture' comes to be seen as product rather than as a process – as an object or thing to be saved rather than as vital, lived action – oral narrative can become disembodied, reduced, simplified and enshrined as something occurring outside daily life. Their work involves painstaking recording of orally performed Tlingit narratives in the Tlingit language following ground rules established with Tlingit elders in the 1970s. And they have gone on to discuss how some of those rules have changed during the intervening decades.

The work that has engaged me for many years in the Yukon draws extensively on the work of the Dauenhauers but may seem to head in different directions, partly because of differing circumstances on the Northwest Coast and in the Yukon interior, as well as because of our different training and life experiences. The elders with whom I worked during the 1970s insisted that their narratives be recorded in English. There are many reasons for this. The Yukon Territory is multilingual, with eight distinct indigenous languages from two distinct language families (Athapaskan and Tlingit). Most individuals born after the construction of the Alaska Highway in 1943 speak English as a first language. In the mid-1970s, when we began this work, there were no Native language programs in place, nor had orthographies been developed for indigenous languages in the region. All this has changed since Yukon Native Language Centre came into being in the 1980s.[1] But during the 1970s, the women with whom I worked had a clear objective. They saw themselves as recording narratives directly for grandchildren who spoke English as a first language, and for whom English in many ways had by then *become* the indigenous language.

For years, it concerned me that the work that engaged us could be considered an example of some of the problems the Dauenhauers have discussed – the distortions that occur when literary narratives originally learned in indigenous languages are told and recorded in English. Over time, though, I've come to the conclusion that when the narrators are in effect their own translators and retain a decisive role in the editing process, even stories narrated and recorded in English continue to be embodied (in the sense that the Dauenhauers use this term) and to have an intense and complex social life in their communities. Repeatedly, I've seen written versions of narratives used as a reference point for reanimating social meanings that might otherwise be erased. In this paper, I want to discuss this issue with reference to three specific examples.

1 Background

First, though, I will begin with some brief background about how I became involved in this work, because editing orally narrated texts is inherently a social process and needs some discussion about how guidelines become established. In the late 1960s, I had an opportunity to go to the Yukon for three months as a young student involved in a small research project. This visit had an enormous impact on me and for a variety of reasons I decided then that I wanted to live in northern Canada and to become involved in work that might allow me to combine what I was learning in school with what I could learn from people I met in Yukon communities, and that might have value at a community level.

I moved to Whitehorse in the early 1970s and, in conversations with politically active indigenous women my own age, questions often arose about whether anthropology had any contribution to make to local research initiatives surrounding Aboriginal claims to land and resources. They suggested that I could make a contribution by recording life stories with their mothers and grandmothers – work that might produce alternative perspectives about the past from those recorded in then standard books about Yukon history. In the 1990s, of course, this kind of work is being done by young men and women with elders from their own communities. Twenty-five years ago, though, young Aboriginal people were beginning to develop organizations that would eventually lead to detailed negotiations crucial for a land claims settlement, and they saw documentation as an appropriate task for an outsider willing to work with direction from elders and their families.

I've had occasion to reflect on these conversations more recently as debates about appropriation of indigenous narratives intensified in southern urban centres during the early 1990s. What is striking in retrospect is that in the Yukon during the 1970s these issues were being discussed all the time, and research protocols were already being carefully worked out. Indigenous Yukon northerners were already extremely sensitive to their situation of double jeopardy during those years – as representing 'north' as well as 'Native' – and we had many animated discussions about developing criteria for what was seen locally as responsible research, writing, and editing long before this was an public issue in southern universities.

At the time, several older women responded to the idea of recording life stories with considerable enthusiasm, and since our initial objective was to produce booklets for the use of families, they wanted their narratives recorded in English so they would be accessible to younger family members. I had no difficulty with this as long as we were recording what might be called secular history, the narratives associated with the goldrush, the early twentieth century fur trade, with the construction of the Alaska highway, the changes brought to women's lives by increasing bureaucratic surveillance during the 1950s. But I *was* troubled when women wanted me to record more foundational narratives in English, again because of what seemed to be the inevitable loss in content that occurs with translation. Furthermore, it seemed to me then that all this was taking us away from what I took to be our primary goal – the documentation of everyday experience. Older women seemed far more interested in having me record complex narratives than in talking about what I took to be their 'life history.'

At their insistence, I continued on their terms, and it was only later when I came to see how they were using these narratives as reference points to talk *about* their life experiences, that I was able to appreciate the complexity of what they were doing. These narratives – about a boy who went to live in the world of salmon; about a girl who married a bear; of men who travelled to the 'other world' in search of a lost sister; or of women who went to live with stars – provided pivotal philosophical, literary and social frameworks essential for providing young and not-so-young people with ways of thinking about how to live life appropriately. The stories erased any distinction between 'story' and 'life.' They were embedded in social life and, in the words of one master storyteller, Angela Sidney, provided guidance about how to 'live life like a story.' Before going on to discuss how narrators demonstrated such connections between narrative and knowledge, I'll return to the theme of our conference by talking about some of the mechanics of editing that absorbed our work during that period.

2 Editing on the page: Problems of translation

In the mid 1970s, then, I began working with senior women from six Yukon communities with the understanding that I would type up their words within a few day of our discussions, returning to their homes as soon as possible so that we could correct, delete, add, eliminate, or change text as they considered appropriate while our conversations were still fresh. Whenever I returned with my transcripts in hand, older narrators usually responded by listening carefully for a short while as I read their words back to them, eventually interrupting to retell the story themselves rather than waiting for me to finish. Because each woman's version was so internally consistent from one telling to the next, this proved an effective method of checking the transcript and allowed me to raise questions about words or topics I didn't understand. Occasionally, they would ask that stories referring to particularly sensitive issues or naming living people be omitted from our transcripts.

Initially, I was quite shy about how much technology to introduce into our work, wondering how older women would feel about the intrusion of a tape recorder. One day, while we were checking a particularly complex narrative, Mrs Rachel Dawson, then in her mid-seventies, asked me whether I had ever thought of using a tape recorder so that I could 'get it right the first time,' thus dispelling any simple notions I had about the alienating effects of technology. During the years we worked together, in fact, the growing use of boom boxes and video cameras by the women's grandchildren made me aware that I was much more inhibited by technology than they were. However, I also found that women's responses to such recording devices varied depending on where we were working. They seemed very much at ease with tape recorders when we worked in their own homes and somewhat more formal whenever we tried to work somewhere un-familiar (in a quiet setting like the Language Centre, selected for its ideal sound-recording potential), complicating my hope that we might produce sound recordings like those described in oral history guidebooks that were simultaneously high-quality and spontaneous.

During the next few years, we prepared family history booklets that I typed, cut, and pasted – we had no computers in those days – and duplicated under their guidance. Our understanding was that the material recorded belonged to the narrator and different narrators made different decisions. In one case, we arranged to have one of the booklets typed on stencils and then duplicated on a gestetner – the best and cheapest technology then available to us – so that Mrs Sidney could sell copies of it at the local post office. A few years later, with encouragement from family members and support from the Council for Yukon Indians and the Yukon Department of Education, narratives by four of the women – Mrs Rachel Dawson, Mrs Angela Sidney, Mrs Kitty Smith, and Mrs Annie Ned – were produced as illustrated booklets under their authorship, with a photo of the author/narrator on the cover of each (Sidney, Smith, and Dawson 1977; Sidney 1982; Smith 1982). With the development of the Yukon Native Language Centre in the early 1980s, we began to focus more on indigenous languages, producing booklets of place names and genealogies, and these, too, were published and distributed under the authorship of narrators (Sidney 1980, 1983; Ned 1984; Tom 1987). As a result of their work, the narrators were invited into schools, on field trips, and to tell stories on radio and on local television. After I returned to graduate school in 1984 to begin my doctoral research in the area of oral tradition studies, three of the older women urged that their work should have a larger audience outside the Yukon, and during the following years, we prepared the collaborative work *Life Lived Like a Story* (Cruikshank, Sidney, Smith, and Ned 1990). By this time, young people were beginning to record narratives with grandparents and other elders in their communities, and we decided to use any royalties to set up a scholarship for Yukon students of First Nations ancestry interested in oral tradition. This scholarship has been awarded annually to a student graduating from high school.[2] Mrs Kitty Smith passed away in 1989, just before that book was published, but Angela Sidney and Annie Ned were each awarded the Order of Canada for their contributions to the documentation of local oral and intellectual history.

The issue of transforming spoken words into written text is complicated, and every time one problem seems to be temporarily resolved, another appears. My initial concern was, again, one raised a century ago by Franz Boas – about the inevitable loss in style and form that occurs when narratives learned in an indigenous language are recorded and transcribed in English. However, if the context of recording has changed during the last two decades, it has certainly changed since

Boas's time, when an ethnographer working with an 'informant' dictated the terms of the research and the language used. A modern-day storyteller working with an anthropologist usually asserts his or her own clear agenda. Although government funding for Native language instruction in Yukon schools has increased enormously since 1980 and sophisticated instructional materials are being developed at the Yukon Native Language Centre, it is still the case that all Yukon Aboriginal children begin school with English as a first language. These women wanted to produce booklets that their grandchildren could read. Their own childhood instruction came either from observation or from oral instruction, but they recognized that children now learn by reading. Mrs Smith, for instance, one day explained her motives for recording her stories by pointing to a great grandchild: 'Well, she's six years old now. She's going to start school now. Pretty soon paper's going to talk to her!' These women saw their narratives as a connection between the world of tradition and the school's 'paper world' and postulated that preparing narratives for inclusion in school programs might be one way to bridge that gap.

A second reason for telling stories in English reflected the developing relationship between each of the women and myself. We worked together for almost two decades and we enjoyed our work enormously. Storytelling does not occur in a vacuum. Storytellers need an audience – a response – if telling is to be a worthwhile experience. Over the years, they patiently trained me to understand indigenous literary conventions so that I could *hear* stories told mostly in English but filled with place names, kinship terms, clan names, personal names in Tagish, Tlingit, Southern Tutchone, and other languages. I also came to realize that each story was told to explain some larger issue to me. The whole rationale would disappear if I could not understand what they were saying.

With the growing interest of younger Yukoners in reclaiming Aboriginal languages, the problem of translation troubled me sufficiently that I went on to work closely with another woman, Mrs Gertie Tom, a Northern Tutchone woman trained by linguist John Ritter, director of the Yukon Native Language Centre, to write her own language. Mrs Tom, in turn, taught me enough of her Northern Tutchone language that I could recognize and transcribe words in that language (and other neighbouring Athapaskan languages). During the 1980s, much of her own work as a Language Specialist at the Centre involved recording elders speaking Tutchone language, then carefully transcribing the tapes. Then she and I would begin a scrupulous word-by-word translation of the story from which we would then rework our verbatim translations into standard English. Gertie Tom has worked with several Tutchone elders recording dozens of stories, many of them long and complex, and the process of learning from her as we translate has been endlessly fascinating. However, we both reluctantly admit that the careful English translations we achieve seem vastly inferior to the original story. English prose flattens out the complexity of Athapaskan verb forms and the finished product lacks the flavour of direct telling that emerges in a narrator's own energetic translation. Stories like the ones Gertie Tom transcribes are critical for linguistic studies, but if no one else is trained to read or hear them, writing them can be a lonely exercise. The elders with whom I worked provided their own translations. Their English is lively, colourful, and highly metaphorical. Although there is undoubtedly something lost, the narrators are at least able to retain their own rhythm, idiom, expressions, and the nuances of their unique narrative performances. To their grandchildren, reading a grandmother's stories 'sounds just like hearing her voice.'

If linguistic subtleties are sometimes lost in such translations, there may be compensating gains in the ways narrators use stories to convey particular messages to unilingual audiences (whether composed of grandchildren or of strangers). The larger issue to which I'll turn now, with specific examples, concerns how storytellers incorporate written English-language versions of their stories into a social process of 'editing in performance.' During years of working with Angela Sidney, Annie Ned, and Kitty Smith, I have come to understand how they see words as having work to do: words *make* the world rather than merely referring to it. From them I have come to appreciate a very particular definition of 'editing' that includes carefully tailoring performances for specific audiences. In the not so distant past, a Native storyteller could always count on local listeners to be familiar with stories they were being told and hence to appreciate why these stories were being directed specifically to them. To really hear a story, these elders agreed, you need to know it already at some level, and if narratives told and written in English can provide today's audiences with background they would otherwise lack, so be it. From this perspective, writing becomes just one more component of performance: one way of familiarizing audiences with narratives so that a storyteller can count on listeners to appreciate the really creative editing or shaping when she tells those stories again. Such a perspective enlarges the definition of performance to include the written page, so that 'editing' goes beyond the written page just as 'performance' may go beyond the physical act of telling the story. Briefly, then, I will summarize three stories about stories told on the printed page.

3 Editing in performance: Translating meanings

1. Angela Sidney's story of *Kaax̱'achgóok*

Angela Sidney was born in 1902 in the southern Yukon to a Tlingit mother and Tagish father. As the eldest daughter in a large family she had opportunities to hear about her bicultural Tagish and Tlingit ancestry, especially when as a young woman she took on the responsibility of caring for her mother, who was plagued with ill health. When we met in the early 1970s, she was eager to work on the project of recording her life story for family members. As she remarked early one afternoon, 'Well, I have no money to leave to my grandchildren; my stories are my wealth.'[3]

I was thrilled to have the opportunity to work with Mrs Sidney on this project. But after we had worked closely together for several months and finally had a 120-page booklet, typed and edited under her supervision, I was somewhat disconcerted by the fact that only about ten to fifteen pages had anything to do with what I would then have called 'life history.' The rest seemed to fall into the category of oral literature which I felt ill-equipped to understand, and uncomfortable about recording in English. But as I continued to listen to and learn from Mrs Sidney, it became clear to me how she was using these larger narratives as reference points to reflect on her own life experiences, as models both for choices she made and for explaining those choices to others. I've discussed how she did this in some detail in the book we prepared together, so here I focus on her use of one story.

Early on, in 1974, one of the stories she asked me to record was about a heroic ancestor remembered by the name of *Kaax̱'achgóok*. Briefly, *Kaax̱'achgóok* was one of the famous Tlingit ancestors of the *Kiks.ádi* clan. One autumn, he went hunting sea mammals with his nephews but soon received a sign that seal hunting was now dangerous for him and that he should return home. Reluctantly, he destroyed his spears and returned to his winter village, but eventually it became unbearable to him that his wives had to beg for food and that they were treated with disrespect. Setting out to sea once again with the same nephews, he was blown off course and became lost. Eventually, the crew washed ashore on a small island. *Kaax̱'achgóok* spent the following months devising ways to feed himself and his nephews, and perfecting a way to plot the sun's trajectory as it moved north, stopping at summer solstice. At precisely the day it reached its zenith, he set sail for home, using the sun as a navigational guide to chart his direction. Despite his successful return, he faced the difficult business of acknowledging how much life had changed during his absence.[4]

When Mrs Sidney first told me this story in 1974, we were both primarily interested in transcribing it in a way that she considered accurate. It subsequently appeared in a booklet by Mrs Sidney and two other storytellers. In elementary social studies classes it was sometimes discussed with reference to summer solstice, and in high school literature classes teachers sometimes compared it with *The Odyssey*.

Several years later, in 1980, I was visiting Mrs Sidney one day when her son, Peter, and his wife arrived. The conversation moved to Peter's experiences as a veteran of the Second World War. He was stationed overseas for a period and Mrs Sidney began to speak about how she had missed him, how she and her husband had bought their first radio so they could listen to news and learn 'where the troops are,' and how happy she was when the war ended and they received a telegram announcing his return. The remainder of her story concerned the plans she made to welcome her son back when he returned home after the war, hosting a community feast and publicly giving him the most precious gift she could – the song Kaax̱'achgóok sang when he returned home after his long absence – a song she then referred to as 'Pete's song' for the rest of her life. As a member of her *Deisheetaan* clan, her son was entitled to receive the song as a gift from her, she pointed out, and she saw it as accurately reflecting the feelings of a man forced to spend an indefinite period away from home and ultimately able to return. As the Dauenhauers have pointed out (1994: 13–15), songs constitute some of the most important property of Tlingit-named clans, and Mrs Sidney was clearly pleased when her husband complimented her on thinking of such a culturally appropriate gift.

But she then went on to tell a third story about this story – the social processes set in motion by her gift. No sooner had she publicly given her son this song in 1945 than she was formally challenged by elders from her father's *Dak̲l'aweidí* clan who disputed her right to sing it – much less give it to her son. They argued that it was the property of the *Kiks.ádi* clan and that her *Deisheetaan* clan had no right to use it. The remainder of her account is the story of how she proceeded with her own research to prove that her use of this story was not thoughtless appropriation but rather a carefully considered decision. She travelled to Skagway, Alaska, to visit Tlingit elders and interviewed them about an incident many years earlier in which a dispute between *Kiks.ádi* and *Deisheetaan* clan members was resolved when *Kiks.ádi* agreed to give this *Kaax'achgóok* song to the *Deisheetaan*. Her story *about* the story confirmed, to the satisfaction of her elders, that she had acted appropriately. Being able to tell this story almost forty years later, in 1980, in the presence of her son (who knew the story well and was a character in it) and to his non-Tlingit wife and to me (both of us familiar with the written text of the narrative) reconfirmed her competence in *using* stories in a socially significant way – and in fact extending her audience once she could make more people understand (through her written version) the connections between a narrative, a song, a gift, and her own ethnographic authority.

A fourth telling was performed for a very different audience, most of them familiar with Mrs Sidney and her role as a master storyteller, but only a few knowledgeable about this particular story. When a college was opened in the Yukon Territory in 1988, Mrs Sidney was asked to be part of the opening ceremonies. This was a thrilling event for many Yukoners because the college means that students can complete part or all of an undergraduate education without having to leave the territory. At this ceremony, Mrs Sidney decided to tell the story of *Kaax'achgóok*. As she described the events to me later (because I was by then a student living away from the Yukon): 'The reason I sang this song is because that Yukon College is going to be like the Sun for the students. Instead of going to Vancouver or Victoria, they're going to be able to stay here and go to school here. We're not going to lose our kids anymore. It's going to be just like the Sun for them, just like for that *Kaax'achgóok*.' But aware that her diverse audience was probably not able to make this connection, she suggested that we should again make available a transcription of the text. We submitted this to the College's journal, *The Northern Review* (Sidney 1988), so that the text with her commentary could be accessible for anyone in the community interested in understanding the connections she was making.

Very carefully, then, Angela Sidney was able to show how a single story can 'do' several different things. She also constructed an important link between an ancient story she remembered, her various written versions of that story, and three distinctly different social occasions – the return of a son, the demonstration of her own deepening knowledge during the 1940s, and the opening of a college in the 1980s. In other words, she was able to edit, in performance, a written version of a narrative that she used as a reference point from which to translate particular meanings to her different audiences. In effect, her work challenges the idea that texts can be 'collected,' because no telling can be separated from the setting, the audience, and the life stage of the narrator.

2. Kitty Smith's carvings of narratives

Mrs Kitty Smith was born in approximately 1890, more than a decade earlier than Mrs Sidney. She, too, was also born into a bicultural family with a Tagish mother and a Tlingit father. Orphaned as a youngster, she was raised by her Tlingit father's mother – an unusual situation in a society where obligations of clan and kinship are traced through the maternal line. We also began working together in 1974. Like Mrs Sidney, Mrs Smith insisted that I record many stories that initially seemed distant from my understanding of her life experience. Like Mrs Sidney, she began much later to talk about critical events in her own life – her mother's disappearance and subsequent death in an influenza epidemic when Kitty was seven or eight years old; her own arranged marriage as a young woman; her later decision to leave this marriage (a courageous decision and one unconventional for a woman from this region in the early 1900s); and her subsequent reunion with her mother's people – members of her own maternal kin group. She then drew heavily on the more foundational narratives she had already recorded to provide explanations for decisions she had made during her own life.

During the years we worked together, Mrs Smith also sometimes mentioned carvings that she had made years earlier. Whenever I asked her about carvings, though, she would shrug off queries about where they might now be – she had sold them or given them away, she said – and would move on to tell stories underlying the carvings. Shortly before she passed away in 1989, however, we learned that some carvings in the local MacBride museum had been made by Mrs Smith. Her granddaughter and another friend arranged with the museum's director for a group visit and when the carvings were brought out, Mrs Smith confirmed which ones were hers. Nearly a century old by then, she was more amused than surprised by this discovery, and not inclined to provide an elaborate narrative about what they 'meant.' Instead, she re-examined her favourite carving, renaming it 'Azunzha-ya' which she translated as 'Got Lost,' enjoying her own joke.

A few years later, in 1992, I asked Mrs Smith's daughter, May Smith Hume, now an elder herself, whether she had ever seen her mother's carvings at the museum. Their existence was a surprise to her, but she recalled childhood memories of her mother carving and expressed interest in visiting the museum with me to see them. With the encouragement of the museum's director, we were able to spend two afternoons examining the carvings and tape recording May's commentary for the museum. She immediately singled out those made by her mother and settled in to talk about them. And like her mother, she retold the stories embodied in the carvings. What struck me immediately was that these were the same narratives Mrs Smith had told herself, several years earlier, to describe critical turning points in her own life.[5]

One carving and story concerns *Dukt'ootl'*, an orphan whose marginal status is vindicated when he is able to perform a task no one else in the community can accomplish, saving both his own life and the lives of other members of the group. The story reflects both the despair and optimism Mrs Smith often expressed about her own childhood as an orphan cut off from maternal kin. A second is the story of *Naatsilanei*, 'the man who made killer whales,' a story she often told to reflect on the dangers of distance from one's maternal relatives when one is forced to live with one's husband's family. In this narrative, a man is abandoned by his opposite moiety brothers-in-law and left to die on an island. He saves himself by the transformative power of carving, fashioning killer whales that carry him back to safety. A third is a carving of the man who abandoned his wife to cohabit with Bear woman, reflecting Mrs Smith's distress when her first husband told her that he was taking a second wife. Her carving shows the man moving toward his bear wife while the human wife carries her child away, leaving the lovers behind.

Especially relevant to our discussion today, each of those stories has been recorded in Tlingit by Nora and Richard Dauenhauer (and in earlier English versions by Swanton, Garfield, and others) and also sculpted on poles from Yakutat to Wrangell. When you juxtapose Mrs Smith's narratives, transcribed in English, and her small carvings, with the narratives recorded by the Dauenhauers and with carvings from Northwest Coast, hers may seem more limited in comparison. Furthermore, without her narrative framework, Mrs Smith's carvings could even be dismissed as 'tourist art' rather than as attempts to edit some of the critical events in her life. But when you juxtapose her 'transcriptions,' in carvings and in words, with her descriptions of her life experience, they become illuminating translation devices: her way of communicating pivotal life experiences to her grandchildren and to a broader audience, for instance the younger English-speaking Yukon

First Nations artists who now look at her carvings and talk about her work. There is something singular about the way she persists in using them as explanatory narratives to edit, translate and make sense of complex personal experiences in culturally meaningful ways.

3. Some current perspectives from Yukon elders

A third example reflects continuing uses of oral narrative by elders a generation younger than the women with whom I worked. On 14 February 1995, the Yukon First Nations Land Claims Settlement Act (Bill c-33) and the Yukon First Nations Self Government Act (Bill c-34) were passed by the Government of Canada. This settlement concludes more than two decades of negotiations that have involved the energies of a generation of Aboriginal people. Among other things, agreements enshrine provisions for joint management of specific programs by First Nations, federal and territorial governments. After generations of Yukon Aboriginal people's exclusion from decisions affecting their social institutions and resources, this seems to suggest remarkable progress. Yet the conceptual categories gaining legal and political force in this process are framed by western concepts and in the English language as 'co-management,' 'sustainable development,' and the ubiquitous 'TEK' (an acronym for 'traditional ecological knowledge'). Even when they share terminology, elders may understand these terms to have meanings very different from those attributed by government negotiators for whom such language is becoming routine.

Indigenous people participating in these negotiations face decisions about how to use the English language. Bureaucratic jargon restricts the range of ways of talking about these issues and narrows available strategies of discourse. If they agree to work within frameworks spelled out in these agreements in order to advance their negotiating position, as they must, they risk losing control of the dialogue. If, on the other hand, they insist on using their own categories and telling their own stories, they may not be understood. Yukon communities are experimenting with this issue in a number of public events, especially at gatherings framed as festivals, a term used to convey both serious intentions and general celebration.

In July 1994, elders from throughout the Yukon came together for an Elders' Festival coordinated by the Elders' Documentation Project, a program originally conceived by the Council for Yukon First Nations (Jensen 1995). The meeting included people of all ages and the expectation was that elders would do most of the talking, giving younger people opportunities to listen. We met on the edge of Teslin Lake, and camped at a comfortable site where meetings, meals, and entertainment were all hosted by Teslin First Nation away from the distractions of town. Of the many issues discussed that weekend, two are especially related to our theme of editing.

At this gathering, a fisheries biologist made a presentation about the contentious catch-and-release program requiring anyone who catches a fish below a specified size to release it back into the water. This program has proven deeply problematic for local elders who speak forcefully about how such practice violates ethical principles because it involves 'playing with fish' that have willingly offered themselves. The biologist, while expressing sympathy with this position, nevertheless explained as clearly as he could the relationship between fish size and future fish stocks, arguing that rational resource use and long term management would ultimately enhance the Aboriginal fishery. An elder disagreed, suggesting that problems with fish stocks were more likely related to disrespectful fishing practices. He then told a story familiar to everyone there, about the Boy Who Stayed with Fish. A youngster, showing hubris by making thoughtless remarks about fish, trips and falls into a river where he is swept into a world where all his normal understandings are reversed. In this world, fish occupy the 'human' domain and all the cultural behavior he has come to take for granted is shown to be foolish and wrong-headed. Gradually, he becomes initiated and properly socialized into his new world and when, the following year, he is able to return to the human world through shamanic intervention, he brings back an understanding of the fundamental relationships enmeshing humans and salmon in shared responsibilities for the health of salmon stocks (See Sidney, in Cruikshank et al. 1990, 75–8, and Smith in the same volume, 208–13, for versions of this narrative). In this context, telling a widely known story – one regularly recorded by elders in booklets – was a way of insisting that native cultural concepts cannot be redefined through western categories like 'co-management' or 'catch-and-release.'

Another topic on the agenda concerned how elders' orally narrated words should be transcribed, an issue long of interest to linguists and students of oral history, but more customarily debated in university classrooms than in lakeside Yukon campsites. The issue put to the assembly was this. Recently, following an elders' conference, a booklet of transcripts had been prepared using verbatim accounts of speeches in English. One reader had objected that 'elders sound unintelligent' when recorded in non-standard English. This group had been asked to make a decision at the present meeting about whether verbatim transcripts of their meeting should be prepared or whether they should be reworked into standard English.

It is important to know that a striking feature of language use in this region has always been the fluid multilingualism that seems to have characterized daily life. If the purpose of language is to communicate, no commitment to this goal can be clearer than in this part of north-western North America where it seems to have been routine in this century for people to speak not just several languages, but languages from different language families. Women like Mrs Sidney and Mrs Smith, for instance, spoke one or sometimes two Athapaskan languages as well as Tlingit, and added English to their repertoire later.

The positions voiced by different elders at this meeting were eloquent and impassioned, and consistently emphasized issues of communication, audience, and connection. One by one, elders spoke about their view that their words, in English, should be transcribed as they were spoken. If the academic concern is one about how recording oral narrative may inappropriately freeze it on the page, the concerns of these elders who spoke during the next two hours were about how words, transcribed as spoken, extend connections – to younger people, to cultural outsiders, to each other – in other words about how they enhance possibilities for communication. Possibly because of recently inscribed land claims settlements, the elders' comments were directed to the written words of lawyers. In the words of one elder, 'We don't want lawyers changing our words. How could we have somebody else change the words – put words in my mouth and change the meaning? It starts from the elder ... from the grass roots. I've never seen a house built from the top down yet ...' Another added (again making reference to lawyers): 'Our elders are our lawyers. To take the work they have done and destroy it by changing it is wrong. They won't be able to read it. What we have done [in preparing the booklets] you have to respect it and be proud of it.' Again, what emerged was a strong sense of commitment to extend communication in whatever forms are possible – writing being only one among many. While everyone would agree that bilingual translations would be ideal, the impossibility of doing that for every Yukon language is recognized.[6] There is also an optimism, expressed at this meeting at least, that English is just one more Native language (and in fact the dominant Native language) – possibly a result of a history of self-confident bilingualism. And there is a shared sense that narratives should be used to dismantle, rather than erect, boundaries.

4. Disembodying text: Truth, technology, and TEK

The unifying theme connecting these three stories about storytelling is the Dauenhauers' proposition that living oral tradition is embodied, and Greg Sarris's similar view that work on oral tradition must be grounded in talk, in dialogue, in interactive relationships where nothing can be fixed (Sarris 1993). I began this paper by saying that two decades of research has left me with more questions about 'talking on the page' than answers and I want to conclude by raising just three.

- What happens when the tradition bearers are no longer living and able to edit, translate, interpret their own narratives in performance?
- What happens when new technologies emerge and such narratives perform their way onto the internet?
- What happens when local knowledge becomes subject to bureaucratic scrutiny?

First, then, the question of changing paradigms. Everyone involved in long-term work in oral tradition inevitably confronts the irony that work during one period with one set of expectations will be evaluated from another set of parameters a generation later. The ground keeps shifting as circumstances change. The energetic thesis animating our oral history projects during the 1970s and 1980s was that gender, age, class, and ethnicity influence the ways people think and talk about their experience, and that community-based projects might challenge conventional ideas about history by documenting varieties of experience. If classic ethnographies with titles like 'The Tanana Indians' or 'The Kaska Indians' written during the 1940s and 1950s seemed to erase any sense of human agency and were often unrecognizable to members of the communities where they were set, our optimistic objective was to show the complexities of life lived during the turbulent decades of the early twentieth century. Our adversary was positivism and our goal was documenting multiplicity. And the elder storytellers with whom I worked certainly taught me to think about those issues in more complex ways than I had imagined.

In academic scholarship during the same period, emphasis in the study of verbal arts shifted from text to performance, from ideas of stability towards lack of closure, from concepts of orderliness to appreciation of variety, from imperial history to critical examination of hierarchies of narratives. But as academics become more comfortable with the constructed nature of all narratives about the past, and with the idea that meanings are not fixed and must be studied in practice, we may disappoint audiences who are asking different questions and searching for a clearer depiction of history, one more consistent with notions of fixity and objectivity than with post-modernism. Increasingly, indigenous communities faced with legal battles want more authoritative versions of metanarratives we hoped to problematize. Given the issues at stake in current negotiations between Aboriginal people and the Canadian state, emerging demands for authoritative 'truth' are understandable and reasonable, if at odds with much contemporary scholarship.

Practicing storytellers like Angela Sidney or Kitty Smith might take an intermediate position if they were still living and able to participate in these discussions. In their work, they repeatedly demonstrated that storytelling contributes to large social processes. It is constitutive rather than referential; in other words, it makes the world rather than merely referring at second hand to disconnected facts 'about' the world. Stories, they might say, are not even really about facts or events; they are about coming to grips with the personal meanings of broadly shared knowledge and converting those meanings to social ends.[7]

As long as living, speaking storytellers can demonstrate how meanings include different audiences and situations, and how listeners become part of their stories, history can be negotiated. In Yukon communities, stories about the past continue to be actively discussed and debated and written versions may carry no more (and sometimes less) weight than spoken versions. But once tellers no longer participate in this process and lose control of editorial performance, their written words may be evaluated as 'data,' often by people who have never heard them speak. Fluidity tends to solidify. The question remains, then, how do the social lives of texts develop and change?

My second, related question concerns new technologies that promise to better reflect the relationship between performance and spoken words than print – electronic media, CD-ROM, the internet, and so on. But again, some of this complicates what happens to carefully edited transcriptions after the narrator is no longer present.

During the last two decades, both in Yukon communities and in classrooms, I've participated in many discussions about the social relations of power involved in the production of tape recorded interviews, and the social relations of representation involved in portraying people in written accounts. A central issue for Aboriginal historians and storytellers involved in such projects concerns who controls the images and representations of lives portrayed locally and to the larger world. There has been a virtual explosion of interest in oral tradition among northern indigenous people working on community-based oral history projects. The annual Yukon International Storytelling Festival has attracted as many as 3,000 people during the summer weekend when it is held. Locally produced plays and videos based on these narratives are being written and performed by Aboriginal writers and actors. The process whereby young people take on, re-embody or reincorporate stories during successive hearings over the course of their lives, making them their own, is one that long preceded writing but one that may be extended by writing when elders are no longer living to tell the stories themselves.

But if the debates that animated recent work are about relations of power and representation, emerging issues may be about relations of *access*. Many current oral history projects receive public funding and tape recordings are usually routinely deposited in archives where they can be preserved under the best possible conditions. Despite restrictions, they may eventually be available to anonymous researchers to use in ways over which the original narrator has no control.

Issues involved in the social relations of editing become more complicated all the time. An increasing number of projects involve putting visual images and words on CD-ROM, sometimes as commercial ventures, further complicating issues surrounding the relationship between narrator and recorder, between archives, researchers, and editors, and cultural copyright of 'documents that move and speak' (Ames 1992). Canada's current copyright legislation makes a distinction between physical possession of a work and exhibition of that work. The idea of cultural copyright – that a group of people has a definite, proper and continuing interest in how their histories, cultures and themselves are to be represented – is an extremely contentious one (Ames 1992: 69–70) and is likely to become more so in an age of electronic media. How, then is copyright to be negotiated after storytellers are no longer living to be involved in decisions about how their words are used?

A third set of questions relates to the editing of indigenous oral tradition once it becomes the object of bureaucratic interest. The idea that indigenous people should speak for themselves rather than be spoken for by others has entered the realm of common-sense discourse internationally (see Myers 1994). In the north, one manifestation of this process is the redefinition of oral tradition as a kind of free-standing 'indigenous science' now playing at least a rhetorical role in public debates. Adding local perspectives to Arctic and Subarctic policy discussions is long overdue; however, the technocratic vortex into which such knowledge is swept may submerge narratives while earnest civil servants claim to learn from them. Management models based on TEK ('Traditional Ecological Knowledge') draw on oral tradition selectively and sometimes seem to drain tradition by codifying it in databases.

A final short story points to the pitfalls involved in trying to reduce indigenous knowledge to databases. Some years ago, a caribou biologist asked whether he could accompany me to visit Mrs Ned. She was living in her cabin thirty miles west of Whitehorse at the time and was pleased that he wanted to consult her. He had heard that she remembered seeing enormous herds of caribou in the southern Yukon during her childhood at the turn of the century. There is archaeological evidence that two subspecies of caribou travelled much further south in the past than they do now.

The biologist was interested in learning what Mrs Ned could tell him about more recent caribou movements and had specific and careful questions he hoped to ask her. She was glad to see him and provided equally thoughtful answers to his questions. When caribou came in winter, she told him, the sound of their hooves could be heard for miles as they clattered across the lakes. On one occasion, large numbers broke through when their weight was more than the ice could support and she described how hard it was for hunters to retrieve the meat and for women to tan hides soaked and frozen in this way. She went on to tell him about one of the last times caribou came in this direction. A man with shamanic powers disappeared when he was taken by caribou. His kinsmen struggled to entice him back to the human world. They could observe what appeared to be a single caribou on the lake, but once they heard it sing this shaman's song, they understood that he had been transformed, and they knew what their obligations were. In a powerful voice, Mrs Ned sang for us the song they heard. Gradually and with great difficulty, through a series of elaborate rituals, people were able to bring the shaman back to the human world even though the transition was immensely difficult for him and he was never again able to hunt caribou (Cruikshank et al. 1990, 336–8). Mrs Ned went on to talk about how this story was bound up with her second husband's powers and the story's significance for his life. Mrs Ned's narrative cannot be easily edited to fit categories of TEK databases. She and her contemporaries would be unlikely to think of such a story as providing 'data,' though they might suggest that listening to it closely could generate different strategies for different listeners, depending on their individual life trajectories. In all likelihood, it would drop out of the database because it confuses rather than confirms familiar categories now becoming routine in the 1990s language of TEK. Yet the local knowledge it conveys about concepts of personhood is being erased in this process.

In summary, I have tried to suggest processes by which Yukon elders insist on editing on the page and in performance and to raise some of the concerns that may accompany the loss of dialogue after the lifetime of a storyteller. Greg Sarris (1993), writing from the position of a Native American who is a professor of literature, gives sound advice on this issue. What is too often missing from Native American studies, he says, is interruption and risk. Academics too often frame the experiences of others with reference to scholarly norms. Yet unless we put ourselves in interactive situations where we are exposed and vulnerable, where these norms are interrupted and challenged, we can never recognize the limitations of our own descriptions. The kind of work we do is grounded in talk, in dialogue, in interactive relationships where meanings cannot be 'fixed.' Academic discourse, he argues, has to be interrogated by other forms of discourse in order to make it clearer what each has to offer the other. It is these dialogues that are most productive, because they prevent us from becoming overconfident about our own interpretations.

NOTES

This paper reflects years of discussion with Mrs Angela Sidney, Mrs Kitty Smith, and Mrs Annie Ned, co-authors in the many projects we have undertaken together during the last three decades. As always, I thank them enormously for what they have taught me and hope that this paper accurately represents the discussions we have had over the years. I thank Laura Murray and Keren Rice for including me in this conference and am especially grateful to Laura Murray for her thoughtful editorial comments and careful questions during the preparation of the manuscript.

1   Under the direction of the linguist John Ritter, the Centre's work targets language instruction in the schools, with less emphasis on the production of literary texts, but the Centre has still managed to produce a substantial list of publications.

2 Winners of this scholarship have been: Georgette McLeod (Dawson City), 1993; Lisa Jacobs (Whitehorse), 1994; Maria Kaye (Old Crow), 1995; and Teresa Waugh (Whitehorse), 1996.

3 This became the title of the first booklet produced as part of this project (Sidney, Smith, and Dawson 1977).

4 This narrative was also recorded by Swanton (1909, Nos. 67 and 101, pp. 225 and 321); and in Dauenhauer and Dauenhauer (1987, 82–107 and notes, 323–33). I have discussed Mrs Sidney's use of this narrative at greater length in Cruikshank and Sidney (1995).

5 Elsewhere I have discussed Mrs Smith's use of these narratives in her carvings and in her account of her life (Cruikshank 1994).

6 Two exemplary publications are by Gertie Tom (1987) and by Elizabeth Nyman and Jeff Leer (1993), both published by the Yukon Native Language Centre.

7 I am indebted to personal communications from David Krupa about similar themes in his work with Peter John, an Athapaskan elder from Alaska.

WORKS CITED

Ames, Michael. 1992. 'Cultural Copyright and the Politics of Documents that Move and Speak.' In *Documents that Move and Speak: Audiovisual Archives in the New Information Age*. Proceedings of a symposium organized for the International Council of Archives by the National Archives of Canada. K.G. Saur: New York.

Cruikshank, Julie. 1994. 'Imperfect Translations: Rethinking Objects of Collection.' *Museum Anthropology* 19, no. 1: 25–38.

Cruikshank, Julie, with Angela Sidney, Kitty Smith, and Annie Ned. 1990. *Life Lived Like a Story: Life Stories of Three Yukon Elders*. Lincoln: University of Nebraska Press, and Vancouver: University of British Columbia Press.

Cruikshank, Julie, and Angela Sidney. 1995. '"Pete's Song": Establishing meaning through Story and Song.' In *When Our Words Return: Writing, Hearing and Remembering Oral Traditions of Alaska and the Yukon*, edited by Phyllis Morrow and William Schneider. Logan, Utah: Utah State University Press.

Dauenhauer, Richard, and Nora Marks Dauenhauer. 1987. *Haa Shuká/Our Ancestors: Tlingit Oral Narratives*. Seattle: University of Washington Press, and Juneau: Sealaska Foundation.

–. 1992. 'Oral Literature Embodied and Disembodied.' In *Aspects of Oral Communication*, edited by Uta M. Quasthoff. Berlin: DeGruyter.

–. 1994. *Haa Kusteeyí/Our Culture: Tlingit Life Stories*. Seattle: University of Washington Press.

Jensen, Marilyn. 1995. 'The Yukon Elders Documentation Project: A Yukon First Nations Oral History Project.' *Northern Review* 14: 21–7.

Myers, Fred. 1994. 'Culture-making: Performing Aboriginality at the Asia Society Gallery.' *American Ethnologist* 21, no. 4: 67–99.

Ned, Annie. 1984. *Old People in Those Days They Told Their Story all the Time*. Compiled by Julie Cruikshank. Whitehorse: Yukon Native Languages Project.

Nyman, Elizabeth, and Jeff Leer. 1993. *Gágiwdul.at/Brought Forth to Reconfirm: The Legacy of a Taku River Tlingit Clan*. Whitehorse, Yukon: Yukon Native Language Centre.

Sarris, Greg. 1993. *Keeping Slug Woman Alive: A Holistic Approach to American Indian Texts*. Berkeley: University of California Press.

Sidney, Angela. 1980. *Place Names of the Tagish Region, Southern Yukon*. Whitehorse, Yukon.

–. 1982. *Tagish Tlaagú/Tagish Stories*. Recorded by Julie Cruikshank. Council for Yukon Indians and Government of Yukon.

–. 1983. *Haa Shagóon/Our Family History*. Compiled by Julie Cruikshank. Whitehorse: Yukon Native Languages Project.

–. 1988. 'The Story of K̲aax̲'achgóok.' *The Northern Review* 2: 9–16.

Sidney, Angela, Kitty Smith, and Rachel Dawson. 1977. *My Stories Are My Wealth*. Recorded by Julie Cruikshank. Whitehorse: Council for Yukon Indians.

Smith, Kitty. 1982. *Nindal Kwädindür/I'm Going to Tell a You a Story*. Recorded by Julie Cruikshank. Whitehorse: Council for Yukon Indians and Government of Yukon.

Swanton, John. 1909. *Tlingit Myth and Texts*. Washington: Bureau of American Ethnology Bulletin 39.

Tom, Gertie. 1987. *Ekeyi: Gyò Cho Chú/My Country: Big Salmon River*. Whitehorse: Yukon Native Language Centre.

PREVIOUS CONFERENCE PUBLICATIONS

1997 *Computing the Edition*, eds. Willard McCarty and Fred Unwalla
(forthcoming)